Other Collier Books by Fred Reinfeld

The Joys of Chess

THE JOYS OF
CHESS

FRED REINFELD

Introduction by Al Horowitz

COLLIER BOOKS
A Division of Macmillan Publishing Co., Inc.
NEW YORK

Collier Macmillan Publishers
London

Contents

Preface

In these addled times, full of tensions and alarms, we concentrate so heavily on the means that we often lose sight of the objectives. To take a very minor instance, we may try so hard to improve our chess that we may lose sight of our objective—to get more pleasure from the game.

The object of this book is to restore that objective—to get more pleasure out of chess. This explains the emphasis on end game compositions and problems. These artistic masterpieces have no competitive features at all, giving them a restful and relaxing quality which adds zest to the solving process.

The beautiful combinations are the highlights of some outstanding games. For those who want to come to the heart of the game without wearying themselves over lengthy sequences of moves, these exquisite sacrificial combinations are ideal.

Why "Brief Candles"? The same principle still applies. If you want to know "where the action is," these short, snappy games will do the trick. One of the players goes wrong early in the game. His alert opponent immediately spots the mistake and exploits it in attractive fashion —the sooner the better.

The "fireworks" games are somewhat longer, but by no means long. These are full-blown games, but the issue is joined quickly, the complications multiply at a breakneck pace, and the conclusion is appropriately lively.

The section on masters' boners will certainly gladden the heart of every average chess player. It is comforting to know that the immortals of the chessboard are occasionally guilty of chess blindness like the rest of us.

The final section by and about chess players is a suitable finale. The masters are as renowned for their foibles and faults as they are for their mighty deeds, and these telling comments will bring many a *chuckle from appreciative readers. And that is precisely the reaction sought in this book.*

FRED REINFELD

Edinburgh, May 1961

How to Record Moves

In order to be able to record moves, we have to give each square on the board a name.

This is how we do it: each of the pieces in the opening position has a specific name. The Bishop next to the King is called the King Bishop. The nearby Knight is the King Knight, and the Rook next to the Knight is called the King Rook.

The pieces next to the Queen are the Queen Bishop, Queen Knight, Queen Rook.

The horizontal row on which these pieces stand is called the *first* rank. Consequently, the square the King Bishop stands on is called King Bishop 1. The square the Queen stands on is Queen 1, etc.

Each Pawn is named for the piece in back of it. Thus the Pawn in front of the King is called the King Pawn and stands at King 2. If it moves ahead two squares, we write the move "Pawn to King 4."

The vertical rows on the board are called "files." They are named for the pieces that stand on them at the beginning of the game. The file the King Rook stands on is the King Rook file. The first square is King Rook 1; the second square is King Rook 2, and so on, all the way down to King Rook 8.

All these details are easy to grasp; but here is a point that troubles many players. White records his moves from his side of the board, while Black records *his* moves from *his* side of the board.

Thus, the square that White calls King 4 is King 5 from Black's side of the board. White's Queen 2 square is Black's Queen 7 square. (Note that these numbers always add up to 9.)

However, if you remember that you must reckon the names of the squares from the side that is making the move, you will have no trouble whatever with the chess notation.

Introduction

by Al Horowitz

To the many thousands of people all over the world who followed from day to day the world championship match in Reykjavik between Boris Spassky and Bobby Fischer, the affair must have seemed a grim business. Whether they watched on television as an assembled panel of experts analyzed each move as it came over the wire direct from the field of battle, or read in the newspapers the lengthy commentary offered by the journalists on the scene, it must have struck them that the two athletic-looking young men were engaged in a struggle if not literally to the death, then to a finish only slightly less conclusive. If the match accomplished nothing else, it did impress the general public with the essential seriousness of chess.

And yet this very seriousness, as manifested in topflight master play, raises some intriguing questions. The problems posed in the course of a chess game are probably among the most complicated the human mind is called upon to solve, but are at the same time in an important sense trivial. They are profound because the game is enormously difficult, and trivial because their correct solution leads to nothing more consequential than victory. Victory may be everything in the context of the game, but outside that context it could hardly matter less. What we learn in the course of the struggle, or in consequence of the result, may increase our knowledge of chess, but of nothing else. Change significantly any of the arbitrary rules that govern the relationships between the pieces on the board, and we would be compelled to start all over again.

Once we allow that victory at chess is merely that and nothing more, those of us who take the game seriously may well feel prompted to examine our attitude more closely. The justification that comes most quickly to mind is the negative one that no justification is necessary: many people take far more frivolous things far more seriously, and often do great harm thereby, both to others and to themselves. Chess may not be good for anything, but at least it keeps us off the streets and out of mischief.

Yet few serious chessplayers would be willing to consider the obscure complications that arise from this line of thought. They have far too great an esteem for their chosen field (not to say of themselves) to admit that chess does not make a more positive contribution to the welfare and glory of the human race, and some have argued their positions very ably. Historically the most popular of these positions has been that chess serves as a training for the mind, that the lessons it teaches its devotees in self-reliance, discipline, foresight, sportsmanship and other sterling qualities can be carried over virtually without modification into Life. This point of view has been most eloquently expressed by no less a personage than Benjamin Franklin in his well-known essay "The Morals of Chess" (1779). "The game of Chess," says Franklin,

> is not merely an ideal amusement; several very valuable qualities of the mind, useful in the course of human life, are to be acquired and strengthened by it, so as to become habits ready on all occasions, for life is a kind of Chess, in which we have points to gain, and competitors or adversaries to contend with, and in which there is a vast variety of good and ill events, that are, in some degree, the effects of prudence, or the want of it.

Much the same claim, with appropriate modifications, has been made to support study of the classical languages, and it is gratifying to recall that chess is ranked by some in the same class with Latin and Greek as a molder of intellect and character.

One is most forcibly disabused of this sanguine attitude toward the game through an acquaintance with chessplayers. While it is hardly likely (one's own last unpleasant experience to the contrary notwithstanding) that chessplayers are any less self-disciplined or sportsmanlike than other people, they are certainly not more so: as in any walk of life, there are some of the highest moral character and others who are downright scoundrels, with most of us somewhere in the middle of the spectrum. Any evidence that chess builds character or trains the mind in any other way is, alas, highly subjective.

Due to certain shortcomings in the argument itself, therefore, as well as to the degeneracy of an age in which it is no longer fashionable to talk about moral, or even intellectual, self-improvement, it is less frequently claimed nowadays than it was when Ben Franklin was one of the leading lights of Philadelphia chess circles that the game is a powerful force for education. At present those who feel moved to demand for chess an exalted position in the hierarchy of human activities usually resort to one aesthetic argument or other: a deeply calculated chess combination, they claim, inspires in the beholder feelings of artistic enjoyment akin to those inspired by a great painting or symphony. A chessplayer, they assure us, is an artist, whose work in his own medium is as important and worthy of respect as that of a painter or musician of comparable stature.

Now this is all very pleasant, and it ill becomes a chessplayer to raise objections. There is little doubt, in fact, that an extremely well-played chess game, or even a single highly imaginative and well-calculated move, can inspire feelings of aesthetic enjoyment in the beholder, feelings in some way akin to those inspired by great works of art, provided the beholder is intellectually equipped to appreciate it. But this is where the analogy breaks down if we try to push it too far: in order to respond to the artistic beauty of a chess game, one must bring to it a far more specialized knowledge than one must bring to a painting or a piece of music in order to respond to it in a similar way. A picture gallery may be a very dull place to a blind man, but anyone who has eyes to see and a certain minimal acquaintance with the conventions of pictorial representation can appreciate the beauty of a great painting. Although the matter is rather more complicated than I have suggested here, it is undoubtedly true that millions of people, some with very little formal education, respond easily to highly sophisticated works of art, and it is even truer of music. A chess tournament, on the other hand, is a very dull place to anybody who doesn't play chess, even if he is a close friend or relative of someone who is competing.

Chess, then, by virtue of the specialized knowledge required to appreciate it, is at some distance from the other kinds of activities we usually think of as making up the world of Art. Indeed, the aesthetic appreciation some derive from chess games or combinations is closer to the feeling inspired by a brilliant exercise in mathematics or formal logic in those schooled to understand and respond to it. As a justification for chess in an absolute sense, the appeal to aesthetics is perhaps most satisfying to those chessplayers who are themselves frustrated painters or musicians.

The fact remains, however, that chess, whether theoretically justifiable or not, is played, and will continue to be played, because it gives people pleasure. Perhaps no one has ever said it better than the great German player Dr. Siegbert Tarrasch (1862–1934), to whom Fred Reinfeld has wisely accorded the last word in the present volume. While the whole of the quotation is justly famous, it is perhaps the last line that is best remembered: "Chess, like love, like music, has the power to make men happy."

While we possess no hard evidence of Dr. Tarrasch's prowess as a lover or a musician, we have eloquent testimonial to his ability as a chessplayer and author; not only through the legacy of his games, for the most part played in a style that is a model of cool precision and logic, but also through his writings, which are justly credited with teaching a whole generation how to play chess. Whatever happiness the good Doctor may have derived from the game, he has repaid in full measure.

And yet there remains something unexplained, and vaguely annoying. Watch the play at an international tournament anywhere in the world, with the players sitting huddled over their respective boards, the inexorable time-clocks ticking away at their elbows, and the audience sitting in hushed expectancy, knowing that the slightest inaccuracy in any of the games will be swiftly and mercilessly punished: the very last thing any of the combatants looks is *happy*. When we remember the protracted wrangling that went on prior to the Spassky-Fisher match, and the atmosphere of tension in which it was conducted, we can hardly bring ourselves to believe that the two opponents were doing it all for pleasure.

Tarrasch himself, who appears within the context of his famous quotation as the apostle of Joy, was in his time the last man in the world one would have dared to accuse of being happy. I have already had occasion to describe Tarrasch as he appeared at the beginning of his first world championship match against Emanuel Lasker, and it is relevant to remember the acrimony with which the negotiations leading up to that match, and the match itself, were conducted (mainly in consequence of haggling over money):

Dr. Siegbert Tarrasch, forty-six years old . . . is in some ways a rather unappealing personality, at least to modern eyes. Certainly he made a pleasant enough impression on most contemporaries: the editor of the Hastings 1895 tournament book describes him as "a man of the highest educational attainments. Visitors to the Congress will remember him as a neat, well-dressed gentleman of very engaging manners, and always with a flower in his buttonhole." It is perhaps this very punctiliousness of dress and manner, as well as his obvious pomposity and sometimes ill-concealed arrogance, that makes him seem to personify the civilian backbone to the Prussian military establishment and all that that implies.*

An anecdote about that match supports this description: Tarrasch and Lasker had not been on speaking terms for years before the match, but an attempt at reconciliation on the part of the organizers brought about a meeting between them just prior to the first game. Lasker, in a burst of magnanimity, put out his hand, but Tarrasch (according to Lasker's biographer, J. Hannak) "made a stiff little bow and exclaimed: 'To you, Herr Lasker, I have only three words to say: Check and mate!' "

Nevertheless, there is no reason to doubt the sincerity of Dr. Tarrasch's attachment to chess, or that, even in the midst of his most exacting tournament and match battles, he was enjoying himself hugely. Why else would the man have devoted so much of his energies to an activity that in his day—indeed, until very recently—offered only the paltriest material remuneration, or that was so often misunderstood by most non-chessplayers. When a brash reporter asked the dour former world champion Mikhail Botvinnik if he liked chess and if he ever regretted that he had started playing it, the old man flashed one of his rare smiles and replied, "Of course I never regretted it. The greatest pleasure is when one feels that he is thinking and that is best accomplished with chess." No doubt Tarrasch and literally millions of chessplayers, ranging in strength from duffers to grandmasters, before and after him, have felt the same way.

What with the vast number of chess books on the market with titles that suggest that mastery of their contents will enable you to

* Al Horowitz, *The World Chess Championship: A History* (New York: Macmillan Publishing Co., Inc., 1972), pp. 57–58.

beat your opponents' brains out, it is a pleasure to introduce one called *The Joys of Chess*. The competitive element is so important in the game, and places such demands on us, that it is good for us to be reminded every so often that the goal of all that competition is enjoyment. And although the element of competition is so important in chess, it is not the only one, by any means. Even if one never played another serious game in one's life, chess is rich enough to afford pleasure to the most casual of its devotees. And the delightful anthology of games, problems, studies and articles offered us by Fred Reinfeld in this volume offers many hours of the pleasure by which chess justifies itself in our eyes.

The Joys of Chess

The World of Master Chess

To the ordinary amateur fascinated but rather cursorily occupied with his hobby, the world of master chess may seem as exotic and remote as space travel. It seems fitting, then, to bring the world of master chess closer to all of us.

We start, not too auspiciously, with an article I wrote several years ago for *Esquire*. The title, needless to say, was not of my choosing and implies a feeling of awe not to say terror toward matters cultural, which the magazine has latterly been striving to overcome.

Chess Men was originally a radio talk inspired in part by my book *The Human Side of Chess*, later republished by Doubleday under the more accurate title *The Great Chess Masters and Their Games*. I think you will agree that Gilbert Highet has treated the subject with a poetic sensibility and reflective insight that make the essay memorable.

During a long and distinguished career Edward Lasker has made himself at home in several worlds, those of chess, science, and music. He has known the great and the near-great in these fields, has enjoyed their friendship, and has described them warts and all in a manner that is endearing and free from malice. I might add that Lasker also has the distinction of having written the first fine chess primer, *Chess Strategy,* for which we all owe him an enormous debt of gratitude.

That the penetrating and highly readable profile of Bobby Fischer was written by an eminent music critic may come as something of a surprise. But Lasker, for one, has amply documented the affinity of chess masters for music, and the affinity of musicians for chess. Not so long ago Abram Chasins told me of Capablanca's love for music and Artur Rubinstein's love for chess. (It oughtn't to be necessary to use Rubinstein's first name for identification; I do it only because of his celebrated countryman, Akiba Rubinstein, one of the noblest artists of the chessboard.)

This affinity is one of the few things Shakespeare failed to allude to, although he does say in *The Merchant of Venice*:

> The man that hath no music in himself,
> Nor is not moved with concord of sweet sounds,
> Is fit for treasons, stratagems, and spoils;
> The motions of his spirit are dull as night,
> And his affections dark as Erebus:
> Let no such man be trusted.

Be that as it may, Harold C. Schonberg, has done a first-class job of describing what it means to be a chess prodigy. Don't be misled by his modest description of himself as "a *potzer* in good standing at the Manhattan Chess Club."

I believe that after you have read these four accounts of the world of master chess that world will seem to you less strange and will seem worthy of closer study.

THIRTY-TWO WAYS TO GO CRAZY*

by Fred Reinfeld

Every chess player knows the story of the Englishman whose friend found him in a very dejected mood.

"My wife threatens to leave me if I don't give up chess."

"Terrible, isn't it?"

"Yes, I shall miss her dreadfully."

It's a mistake, though, to think that the fascination of chess keeps the great masters from pursuing regular careers in the business or professional world. One of the outstanding American players is a leading editor; another, a former U. S. Champion, is in the meat provision business. Accounting, psychoanalysis, pharmacy and teaching are all represented by chess masters. Among the recent World Champions, Emanuel Lasker was a mathematician, and José Raoul Capablanca was in the Cuban diplomatic service; Alexander Alekhine had two degrees in law, and Max Euwe was a teacher, an excellent

* Copyright 1953 by Esquire, Inc. Reprinted from *Esquire*, March 1953.

swimmer and boxer, and a flier. Many of them don't look like chess masters, either. In his youth Capablanca's stunning good looks ran him a close third to Rudolph Valentino and Ramon Novarro, and the three best players in Holland are Euwe, Prins and Donner—all solidly over six-foot three.

Most people think that chess mastery takes a lot of study, but the big guns have won their places in history with fantastic ease. Capablanca was never even taught the moves. At the age of four he watched his father playing chess, and on his third run as kibitzer he began teaching Dad the fine points. Sammy Reshevsky was giving simultaneous exhibitions—playing anywhere from twenty to forty opponents at once—all over Europe and America when he was seven and eight years old. Paul Morphy, who was born in New Orleans in 1837, was able to lick all comers at the age of ten. He was American Champion at twenty, went to Europe and crushed the best opposition, then returned to the U.S.A. and never bothered to play serious chess again.

There is nothing special about the chess mind: it blends with almost any profession. Max Harmonist, a pretty good player in his day, was a ballet dancer; Ignatz Kolisch, a nineteenth-century master with a dashing style of play, became a millionaire financier (chess helped him—he played with bankers and such and picked up market tips); Johannes Zukertort, one of the greatest players of his day, knew twelve languages, had a university degree in medicine, served with distinction in three Prussian wars, was an authority on philology, theology, music, politics and prison reform, an outstanding fencer and pistol shot, and a master at dominoes and whist.

The game can be hard work. Some games in serious competition have lasted twenty hours, and the average tournament or match game runs about five hours. Players are required to make forty moves in two and a half hours—a total of five hours altogether—and the player who runs out of time automatically forfeits.

It is possible to win a game of chess in as little as two moves on each side, by the Fool's Mate, which is centuries old and has had untold thousands of customers. Even among the masters games are sometimes very short. Arthur Dake of Portland, Oregon, took a plane to San Francisco in 1929 to play World Champion Alekhine—and lost in thirteen seconds. Three years later he met the World Champion again, this time in a big international tournament, and beat him.

Time control introduces a tricky element into master chess. When

Reshevsky played Capablanca in a tournament in 1938, Capablanca took two minutes for his first ten moves while Reshevsky took fifty-eight minutes. Now Capablanca had plenty of time for his remaining moves, whereas Reshevsky had to step briskly to avoid losing on time.

One of the favorite diversions of chess players is "rapid-transit" chess—played at the rate of ten seconds a move, fourteen minutes for a forty-move game. The chess in such a contest can be remarkably good. Reuben Fine has gone a step further, playing as many as four games simultaneously—blindfold—at the rate of ten seconds per move.

The first requirement for a chess master is a superhuman memory. Take the performance of the late Frank Marshall, who played 155 games simultaneously in Montreal in January 1922. In this exhibition Marshall, who was U. S. Champion for many years and once made a move so astonishing that spectators showered the board with gold coins, won 126 games, lost only eight, and drew twenty-one. He was then in his early fifties, and to many the most astonishing part of his performance was the walking around. Yet Marshall took very little time for this mammoth performance: only seven hours and fifteen minutes—an average of three minutes per game.

Back home in New York a week later, Marshall was able to play over 153 of the games from memory. He was disturbed about forgetting the other two—he felt he was losing his grip.

The chess master's phenomenal combination of memory and imagination is shown most spectacularly in blindfold play, when the master plays without sight of the board or men, remembering his opponent's every move (called out to him by an assistant) and his own position. There are thirty-two pieces and sixty-four squares on a chessboard; and the memory difficulties involved can be illustrated by the fact that there are 169,518,829,100,544,000,000,000,000,000 different ways of playing the first ten moves.

The world's record for blindfold play is forty-five simultaneous games, played by Miguel Najdorf at São Paulo, Brazil, in 1947. The exhibition took almost twenty-four hours, and the blindfold master won thirty-nine, lost only two and drew four.

Blindfold play was first reported in 1266, and probably goes back even further; but we still have no clear-cut explanation of what makes the thing possible. We do know that the masters have amazing memories for facts outside as well as in chess. Once before an exhibition, for example, Harry Pillsbury, an American master at the turn of the century, was shown the following list of words:

antiphlogistine	Freiheit	Piet Potgelter's
periosteum	Philadelphia	Rost
taka-diastase	Cincinnati	Salmagundi
plasmon	athletics	oomisillecootsi
Threlkeld	no war	Bangmamvate
Streptococcus	Etchenberg	Schlechter's Nek
Micrococcus	American	theosophy
Plasmodium	Russian	catechism
Mississippi	philosophy	Madjescomalops

Pillsbury went through the list, put it away and then rattled off all the words, first in their actual order and then in reverse—flawlessly each time, of course. Twenty-four hours later, without having seen the list again, he could still rattle off the words without a hitch!

Pillsbury apparently operated on the principle of visual memory: he had the image of each complete position before him as his mind went from one game to another. Some masters, however, work not by *memory* but by *recall*. They forget each game as they pass on to the next one; but, by recalling all the moves made, they arrive at the current position on each board. They do it without a mistake, and so quickly that there is no perceptible hesitation.

The great Alekhine made use of a modified recall system. He claimed that as each opponent called out his move, the timbre and unique quality of the individual's voice summoned up the position on the chessboard. Whatever the system, though, only the most intense concentration will make it work.

Right now chess is slightly menaced by a less attractive chess-playing machine. Dr. Norbert Wiener of M.I.T., the founder of cybernetics, believes that some of the new electronic brains could be taught to play the game. The prizes for chess victory have run all the way from half a pound of butter (in 1916, in blockaded Germany) through money and fame (Steinitz and Capablanca had horses named after them) to thirty-two beautiful young virgins used as living pieces and awarded to the winner (by Akbar, the famous ruler of ancient India). No machine could beat a man with a prize like that at stake.

CHESS MEN[1]

by *Gilbert Highet*

To be great, to be a champion, a Nobel Prize winner, a supreme
virtuoso, must be a strange and painful experience. Difficult it is,
certainly, difficult beyond the imagination of most of us. Such people
live lives far more intense and far more directed than we do. We are
like a fire of leaves, burning in the garden, sending up pleasant smoke
and making a friendly color and doing a domestic duty. They are like
blast furnaces. If we could see into their hearts, we should be blinded.
If we were exposed to the full heat which they generate, we should be
shriveled.

It is one of the best reasons for reading the biographies of remarkable men and women: to see how much power they produced, and how
much endurance they manifested; yes, and how many resources they
could call on in an emergency—resources hidden even from themselves.
But there is another reason, which may not appeal to so many of us,
though it is still valid. This is that, in some fields at least, greatness
appears to be closely allied to madness, and that it is sometimes necessary to decide whether one wants to be normally happy at the price of
remaining mediocre, or to be great at the price of venturing outside
the frontiers of calm well-being, perhaps of comprehensible, controlla-
ble life.

In the small, flat world of the chessboard, there have been a number
of remarkably great men. You feel that, if they had directed their
talents and their will power in other directions, they might have become great discoverers or powerful philosophers.[2] Their biographies
are full of wildly romantic incidents; their characters fairly bristle with
eccentric individuality. So do their games. You know how easy it is
to tell, in music, the clear, hard, intellectual piano tone of Claudio
Arrau from the delicate, feathery lightness of Walter Gieseking. In
the same way, when you play through a game by one of the great

[1] Copyright © 1957 by Oxford University Press, Inc. Reprinted by permission.
[2] That may not be true, of course. Certainly the converse does not hold. Chess
is a war game; but Napoleon, one of the greatest soldiers who ever lived, a superb
strategist and an unequaled tactician, has been charitably described (by H. J. R.
Murray in his *History of Chess*) as "a poor but persistent chess player."

masters of chess, it is quite as easy to recognize and appreciate the crystal clarity and economy of the Cuban genius Capablanca, the tough, unforgetful, grasping, defensive approach of Steinitz, the desperate gambler's brilliance of Alekhine. And it is not hard to connect these three styles with the individual characters and histories of the three men: Alekhine, the exiled Russian, who lost two fortunes, and who not only lost the world championship but, in an unprecedented feat of energy, recovered it again; Capablanca, the handsome, exquisitely polished Cuban, who was a diplomat by profession, and whose finest games recall the delicate negotiations of a treaty in which one power, almost without force, imposes its will upon another; and Steinitz, who lived all his life in grinding poverty, had to make his way against almost every conceivable obstacle, was crippled for much of his life, and died penniless.

It is easy to envisage the chess masters as remarkable individuals; and an excellent book by Fred Reinfeld called *The Human Side of Chess* (published in 1952 by Pellegrini & Cudahy)[3] tells the life stories of eight of the greatest, adding some of their most characteristic games.

The strangest of them all was surely the American genius Paul Morphy, who is a subject not only for chess study but for psychoanalysis. Morphy was born in New Orleans in 1837, was a child prodigy at the game, and easily won the first American chess championship at the age of 20. Then he went on to Europe, in order to establish his reputation and the reputation of American chess there by defeating the leading European players. He cut down the immortal Anderssen and several others; but, by a disgusting series of rude and underhand maneuvers, the chief British chess authority, Howard Staunton, managed to avoid playing him in a match, and he returned to the United States not only depressed but embittered. When he reached his home in New Orleans, he issued a challenge to any player in the world, offering the heavy odds of a pawn and a move. There was no reply. At the age of 22, Morphy gave up chess forever. During the Civil War he did not fight on either side, but asked for a diplomatic appointment, which was refused. He and his family then fled to Cuba and, even farther, to Paris, returning only when the war ended. He tried to follow the career for which he had been designed, the law; but he was slowly going mad, with severe

[3] *Editor's Note:* Later republished by Doubleday under a new title—*The Great Chess Masters and Their Games.*

seclusion mania and paranoia. At the age of 47 he died, apparently of a cerebral hemorrhage, and was released from years of the most miserable unhappiness, concealed only by his exquisite dress and manners.

Now, it is possible to explain this sad and curious career in different ways. Do not forget that in those days, a century ago, Americans often felt socially and culturally inferior to Europeans. Morphy was one of those who endeavored to redress the balance by proving that America could produce geniuses quite as brilliant and gentlemen quite as cultured as any country in Europe. In this he both succeeded and failed: succeeded, because the French and other western European societies gave way to his skill and his charm; failed, because the English dictator of chess, Howard Staunton, not only avoided a direct meeting with him, and refused to answer his letters, but snubbed him in the most brutal way, hinting in his chess column that Morphy was a crook who played chess as a method of swindling people out of their money. (Staunton's own behavior is partly explained by the fact that he was reputed to be the illegitimate son of an earl.) But also, in New Orleans, chess had been a game for gentlemen. In Paris and elsewhere Morphy saw that professional chess players were too often miserable wretches who spent their lives in cafés where they would play anybody, however unworthy, for a dollar. This horrified him. It horrified his mother even more. On his return to New Orleans, although he was virtually the champion of the world, she begged him to take a solemn promise that he would never again play in public. Perhaps, then, Morphy's rejection of chess was a social rejection: he had found that gentlemen did not play chess—or at least did not play chess well.

Another possible explanation has been given by the biographer and pupil of Freud, Dr. Ernest Jones. (This can be found in a long essay on Morphy reprinted in Jerome Salzmann's *Chess Reader,* published in 1949 by Greenberg.) Jones points to the peculiar character of the game of chess. It is a game of war, in which the aim of each party is to kill the other's king. "Checkmate" means "The king is dead"—so that now there is only one king left alive on the board. Freudians interpret this as a symbolic attempt to kill the father, even when he is defended (as he usually is) by the queen-mother. Dr. Jones goes on to point out that Morphy's brilliant career as a world champion began just a year after the unexpected death of his father, and that it may therefore be a reaction to that critical event, comparable to the most wonderful of all father-killing tragedies, Shakespeare's *Hamlet*. If that is true, then the elderly and unapproachable Staunton, Morphy's British opponent, would become the next symbol of a kingly father who had to be destroyed. When Staunton not only refused to meet Morphy, but kept him at arm's length, treating him as a child, Morphy renounced chess altogether—seeing that it was (in the words you must never use to any chess enthusiast) "only a game," a symbolic solution to real-life situations, and therefore an escape from them.

Now, this may sound fantastic. Many theories of psychology seem to be fantastic, and yet they are explanations of the activities of the subconscious mind—which is the creator of fantasy, our defense against reality. Still, it seems to make good sense in one important way. This is that chess is a constant war. Every chess master is trying to destroy every other. Therefore, we should not consider them as individuals, but rather as parts of couples, some real, some imaginary. Compare them with creative artists. A composer is usually engaged in writing music which he hopes will say all that he has to say, and will last; he is not usually in bitter knife-to-knife competition with some other eminent composer. But a chess player of the master class is either on his way up, or on his way down. All the other men of his generation are either his victims or his rivals; the younger men are his dangers. The world champion . . . he seems to be happy, poised and confident. In fact, he is like the solitary king combined with the queen. He is the master piece, with more than the mobility of the master piece; but against him there is ranged a formidable mass of opponents: shrewd bishops, lively unpredictable young knights, stolid rooks who can clear a path to his very door with one artillery blast, and many faceless little pawns, any one of which may advance far enough to pinion him, or to kill him. Perhaps that is why there are scarcely any good women chess players. Women compete with one another openly, on real issues—looks, dress, manners, love of family; then they stop. But men compete all the time, often in purely concealed or symbolic competitions, in fields like mountain climbing, chess and money-making.

This helps to explain some of the oddities both in the behavior and in the play of the chess masters, not only at present, but far back into the past. They have all been fighting either one single man whom they knew well, or else a vague, nameless, still dangerous murderer stealing up behind them. They have been like the priest in Diana's grove at

Nemi, "the priest who slew the slayer, and shall himself be slain."
Therefore chess is not an art like other arts. It is a duel. Students of the
game sometimes forget this. As they sit at the quiet table, with the
analysis of some famous game in front of them, replaying the moves
on their own board, they view it as though it had been the undisturbed
activity of two minds, while in fact it was the deadly conflict of two
personalities. In one game, a player had to ask for a separate table because his opponent (Steinitz) disturbed him by slurping his lemonade
so loudly. Another game was lost by Lasker because his opponent in-
sulted him by reading Nietzsche between moves. In his turn,
Nimzovich lost to Lasker because he hated tobacco and saw Lasker
holding a fat cigar. He complained to the director of the contest, and
the director genially pointed out, "Dr. Lasker hasn't even lit his cigar.
He is not smoking." "I know, I know," cried Nimzovich, "but he is
theatening it!"

A few of the masters have felt it their duty to conquer the past before
approaching the present; thus Akiba Rubinstein is believed to have
memorized all the master games of previous years before beginning his
career. Others, isolated on the pinnacle of eminence, have lashed out
all around them with pronouncements so universally spiteful as to dis-
courage all past and present and future opponents. A few, like
Alekhine, have escaped from the unendurable loneliness into drink and
drugs. The most brilliant and unpredictable of all chess masters,
Emanuel Lasker, could find (or admit) no worthy opponent among
his contemporaries. So he invented one. It was not Capablanca, or
Steinitz, or any of the human foes whom he had defeated. It was a
monster, a super robot, who could not make a mistake, who could think
through all the billion possibilities involved in every move, subject them
to comparative analysis, and choose the best. He called the creature the
Machéid, which he intended to mean the Son of Conflict, the ultimate
result of a kind of natural selection which has scarcely yet begun—the
natural selection of the most intelligent, through competition and
elimination. Perhaps IBM is even now working on such a super robot.
Surely several of the machines now available could at least analyze the
chief queen's pawn openings as far as four or five moves. Will their
descendant be able to work out perfect middle games, and to solve
final problems? If so, we shall have to devise a more difficult game than
chess. Man must still compete with man, and not with man's creation.

REMINISCENCES OF THE GREAT MASTERS
OF OUR ERA*

by Edward Lasker

From the viewpoint of the chess historian, I was very fortunate in that the accident of my birth made me a contemporary of the three world champions who dominated the chess scene in the first four decades of this century. They were the German, Dr. Emanuel Lasker; the Cuban, José Raoul Capablanca; and the Russian, Alexander Alexandrovich Alekhine. I became intimately acquainted with all three of them, as opponents across the chessboard and as human beings.

Emanuel Lasker had won the world title by defeating Steinitz in 1894 in New York. After fourteen years of residence in the United States he returned to his native country to marry the sweetheart of his college days. I had been looking forward with awe and excitement to meeting him. I was a young student in Berlin at the time, and Lasker, naturally, was my hero. My father had shown me the game of chess when I was a boy of six, just because he had read reports of the great chess victories of our namesake abroad, and I had, of course, resolved to become a chess champion too. I had not been able to establish a family relationship, but after making Lasker's acquaintance I found that, quite apart from chess, there were many other interests which bound us together more strongly than family ties. As a matter of fact, on the many occasions when we met, in thirty-three years of unbroken friendship, he very rarely talked about chess. When he did do so, I always learned a great deal. No matter what subject he discussed, he brought to it an interesting, original point of view.

By training he was a mathematician. But while mathematics remained his main interest throughout life, he gave it up, as a means of livelihood, in favor of chess because, being of Jewish descent, his chances of obtaining a professorship at a German university were practically nil. Besides, as he once told me with a smile, there was another good reason: "In mathematics, if I find a new approach to a problem, another mathematician might claim that he has a better, more elegant solution. In chess, if anybody claims he is better than I, I can checkmate him."

He did teach mathematics for some time in England. Also, he wrote a book in the field of algebra, which several leading mathematicians have told me was highly original. In fact, one of them said he felt it was the best book on the subject.

Lasker's pet idea was the application of mathematics to philosophical problems. In 1908 I introduced him to the famous philosopher Ernst Cassirer, a distant relative by marriage and a frequent chess antagonist of mine. The three of us often took long walks in Berlin's Tiergarten, in the course of which Lasker developed his thoughts on the possibility of attacking the problem of free will by purely mathematical induction. Cassirer told me, in private, that it was obvious Lasker was not very familiar with philosophical literature, so that frequently he did not realize that others before him had come to the conclusions he propounded. But there was no question that Lasker had highly original and interesting ideas on philosophical problems, worthy of publication. In 1913 Lasker actually did publish a philosophical book, entitled *Das Begreifen der Welt (The Understanding of the Universe)*. In it he deals with the age-old problems of reality, causality, cognition, truth, and logic within a mathematical frame, and his contribution to philosophical literature was acknowledged to be decidedly noteworthy.

On the subject of chess Lasker wrote comparatively little, but what he did write was again thoroughly original, and it was distinguished by the attempt to arrive at scientific generalizations which he felt must be applicable to chess to make it worthy of interest to the mature mind. All of his works more or less amplify the thoughts he had originally expressed in a little book called *Struggle,* in which he had tried to develop a number of general strategic principles as guides in any competitive activity, whether chess, or boxing, or business, or war, or life itself.

Lasker had an extraordinary fighting instinct which, in chess tournaments, made him dangerous to his strongest opponents even when he had got himself into hot water through his love for experimenting with new moves. He saved many a lost game by complicating the situation to such an extent that, under the pressure of the time limit, his opponent went wrong.

He once remarked that one of the secrets of chess was never to make a move which was purely defensive. It should always involve a threat, no matter how slight. He added that a threat usually disconcerted an adversary more than its execution. This remark led to an amusing scene in a tournament in which one of Lasker's opponents had obtained his promise that he would not smoke during the game, because, absorbed in thought, he was wont to blow the smoke directly into his antagonist's face. After five or six moves Lasker pulled a long cigar from his pocket and put it in his mouth. His opponent jumped up and called the tournament director to the table. "Lasker agreed not to smoke," he protested. "But he isn't," the umpire pointed out. "His cigar is not lit!"—"Ah, but he *threatens* to smoke," the other wailed, "and you know very well how he values a threat!"

True to the ideas which Lasker had expressed in *Struggle,* he viewed the conduct of a chess game against a master primarily from the standpoint of justice. He conceded that he had no right to expect he should have a winning position as long as his opponent had not violated any of the principles of chess strategy or committed a tactical error. That is why he never made the mistake of trying to force a win in a clearly drawn end game. He considered it almost unethical to continue such a game in the hope that the opponent might make a blunder. There were a good many other masters, notably Janovski, who, on principle, never accepted the offer of a draw. They either suffered from a chronic delusion that their position was always superior, or, for some unaccountable reason, they considered it likely that the other player would make a bad mistake but that such a thing could not happen to them.

Lasker attempted to win an even position only when he saw a possibility of complicating the game from the strategic viewpoint. He never assumed that his opponent might not be able to calculate combinations as accurately as he could do it himself. But he would pose subtle positional problems, which, even for a master, were no easy matter to solve. He was an excellent chess psychologist and knew how to steer a game into channels which did not suit his opponent's style of play.

The world title remained in Lasker's hands for fully twenty-seven years! Even though he lost it, at the age of fifty-two, to José Raoul Capablanca, who was twenty years his junior, he finished ahead of Capablanca in several later tournaments. In one of these he accomplished that feat although he was sixty-six years old!

Like Capablanca, Lasker hardly ever looked at a chess book, relying, rather, upon his ability to find over the board the best move in any new opening variation with which an opponent might confront him. However, by the end of the first quarter of this century, a crop of younger masters had amassed such a vast amount of knowledge in so-called *modern* openings which they themselves had invented and thoroughly analyzed, that ignorance of these analyses proved to be a great disadvantage even for a Lasker.

He realized this himself only too clearly. A few days before the start of the great New York International Masters' Tournament of 1924, he told me, during a walk in Central Park, that he did not think much of my chances in that tournament; nor, for that matter, of those of any other participant, including himself, who had not familiarized himself with the doings of the "New School." He said: "In a tournament game, where you are limited to two hours for your first thirty moves, you will be lost from the start against any of these young fellows [he meant Alekhine, Réti, Bogolyubov, et cetera] if you cannot avoid being drawn into one of their modern openings. Let us even assume you find the best line of play over the board, and it takes you only thirty minutes to do so. They have studied these openings day and night for the last six years. Against your thirty minutes they will consume no more than five—and how can anybody give a first-class master the odds of twenty-five minutes?"

Lasker won the tournament all the same, and the amusing though erroneous comment of a chess columnist was: "The New School came, saw, and succumbed." The real reason was that despite his age Lasker still had extraordinary powers of endurance, so that the contest did not exhaust him physically to a degree where he blundered through fatigue.

The one blunder he made in the tournament was due to time trouble. This was in one of the games with Capablanca, in a position which, ordinarily, he would have drawn with ease.

In this game a scene occurred which shows how a perfectly genial disposition can go to pieces in a chess contest when the relentless clock adds to the nervous strain a tournament player has to endure in any case. Lasker, if anything, had a more kindly attitude than normal among chess antagonists. But he completely lost control of himself when, forced to make nine moves in less than two minutes, he made a bad mistake which lost the game.

Capablanca also had been pressed for time, but it had seemed to Lasker that the minute hand on his opponent's clock was traveling more slowly than his own. In his excitement he not only accused the tournament committee of negligence in testing the timing equipment before the start of the tournament, but he insinuated that one of the committee members who was partial to Capablanca had purposely adjusted his clock so that it would run a little slow. He pointed out that more than four hours had elapsed when the two clocks showed two hours each, and he concluded that someone had "fixed" Capablanca's clock—something he would not have dreamed of in a normal frame of mind.

When Lasker entered this tournament he was definitely conscious of the handicap which his age imposed upon him. The playing schedule called for two sessions of four hours each, five days a week, with adjourned games played off on the remaining two days if necessary. To guard against excessive fatigue, Lasker's matchless incompetence in practical matters made him resort to the strangest means. It never occurred to him that fresh air and a daily brisk walk were the best aids in keeping himself fit. In fact, he argued with me one day that an atmosphere of semisomnolence—readily induced, I could not help thinking, by the dubious brand of cigars he smoked incessantly—was probably more conducive to good chess than fresh air. He went on to explain that sustained concentration created a poison in the blood stream which, in younger years, the body combated effectively by producing more than the normal amount of phosphorus. Older people had to aid this phosphorus production by proper diet, which meant eating a good deal of fish. After winning the tournament, he was not to be dissuaded from his belief that his dietary management had had much to do with his victory.

As long as I knew Lasker I never ceased to wonder how he could stand up under the terrific strain of match and tournament play despite the unreasonable hours he kept even when no professional duties prevented him from going to bed before 3 A.M. He never carried a watch, because he "did not want to be tyrannized by Time." He ate when he felt hungry, and he slept when he felt tired. Synchronizing lunch or dinner engagements with him was therefore quite a task. Whenever I had arranged to meet him, I took the precaution of postponing all other engagements planned for the day.

Lasker was an intellectual, and conversation with him always turned, as a matter of course, into a serious discussion of one abstract problem or another. But he possessed a healthy sense of humor and had many an amusing story to tell, particularly about people who, unaware of his identity, would ask him to play chess with them.

On the first day of an Atlantic crossing, while walking through the smoking saloon, Lasker saw a man seated alone at a chess table, pondering a position. In passing the table Lasker casually glanced at the position, and the stranger asked him whether he played chess. "Oh, once in a long while," Lasker replied truthfully. "Well, sit down and play a few games," the other said. "I play a good deal, and we can make up for your lack of experience by a handicap. I'll give you Queen odds in the first game. If you win, we'll make it Rook odds, and so on until we find our relative strength." "That's all right with me," Lasker replied, planning to give the man a little lesson.

He let him win the first game quickly, testing his strength, and then managed to lose a second game without causing any suspicion in his opponent's mind. When it came to the third game, Lasker said: "There must be some advantage in playing without the Queen. Perhaps because the King has more freedom of movement when the space next to him is not occupied. Let me give *you* the Queen this time. I think I will do better then."

The other laughed: "But how absurd! I beat you twice with Queen odds, and you want to play me without *your* Queen! That really would be too ridiculous!" But Lasker was stubborn, and the man had to give in. Naturally Lasker beat him. Somewhat flustered, his opponent explained: "Well, I did not really pay very careful attention. Perhaps I took you too easy after all. Let's play an even game now." No, Lasker insisted on giving him Queen odds again, and again he won. This time his opponent no longer knew what to say. But he discovered what a fool he had made of himself when he found Emanuel Lasker's name on the passenger list.

Lasker was the hero of the great masses of chess fans of his time, but he had few friends among the officials of chess organizations and among the editors of chess columns and chess magazines in his native country. His all-encompassing mind lifted him high above mere chess specialists. They did not comprehend him, nor did he seek their company. The result was that he did not have much active support from influential chess friends when he fought the officials of the German Chess Federation, who objected to the size of the purse he had asked for playing a match with the world championship at stake.

Like its counterparts in too many other countries, the German Chess

Federation was run by politicians who were mainly interested in their own glory. For them this meant getting re-elected every year as president and vice-president, and thus surrounding themselves with the nimbus of authority. Since more votes come from mediocre players than from masters, these politicians would always cater to the little vanities of local chess talent rather than make an effort to advance the cause of master chess.

When they derided Lasker because he had stipulated a fee of two thousand dollars for playing in any tournament, and had asked ten thousand dollars for himself out of the purse to be raised for a world championship contest, he reminded them that his predecessor Steinitz, the first world champion, had died in poverty; and he added that he would do all in his power to raise the financial status of professional chess masters throughout the world.

He won his point. When he consented to play Capablanca for the title in 1921, he was paid the fee which he had stipulated. In German money this was a fortune at the time. But fate did not favor him. In the fantastic inflation of 1923, which devaluated the German mark until it was worth less than a fraction of a cent, Lasker lost everything he had and, at the age of fifty-five, had to make a fresh start. Before retiring from the tournament arena in 1936, he won the first prize in the New York tournament of 1924, the second prize at Moscow in 1925, and fully ten years later, again at Moscow, he finished third in a long list of first-class masters. Indeed a triumphant career! In all he competed in twenty-one tournaments. He won twelve of them, was second four times, and finished below third place only on three occasions, two of these being his last tournaments, which he played in Moscow and Nottingham at the age of sixty-seven.

Lasker engaged in twenty-two individual matches, in twelve of which he did not allow his opponent a single game. He also won all the others, except his last match, after which Capablanca succeeded him to the chess throne.

Lasker's fame transcended the world of chess. Anyone who could read was apt to know his name, whether he played chess or not. The publicity attending Lasker's victories stimulated chess interest everywhere, and first-class chess masters developed in ever-increasing numbers. Among the most famous contemporaries of Lasker were the Americans Harry Nelson Pillsbury and Frank J. Marshall, the German Siegbert Tarrasch, the Austrian Carl Schlechter, the Frenchman (of

Polish birth) David Janovski, the Hungarian Géza Maróczy, and the Polish-Russian Akiba Rubinstein.

In the first international tournament in which Pillsbury participated, at Hastings in 1895, he finished ahead of Lasker. But he never duplicated this feat and so did not come into consideration as contender for Lasker's crown. His world-wide fame was mainly due to his extraordinary blindfold performances, which surpassed anything that had ever been accomplished by others. In the same time that Morphy had consumed for eight games, Pillsbury played twice that number. On one occasion he took on sixteen chess games and four checker games simultaneously, at the same time playing whist.

I was a schoolboy, passionately devoted to chess, when Pillsbury toured Europe in 1902, giving almost daily large blindfold exhibitions. On this tour he also came through my home town. The men in charge of arrangements had permitted me to take a board, but my mother forbade me to go out in the evening to play chess. Little do mothers know what an all-consuming fire the passion for chess can be. After brooding all day over the tragedy into which my mother was about to turn my life by preventing me from playing with the famous chess star, I ran away from home!

The terrific mental strain entailed in these forced performances of blindfold chess did not fail to make themselves felt in Pillsbury's state of health. When he played in the International Masters' Tournament of Cambridge Springs, in 1904, he no longer had the necessary endurance and, for the first time in his career, he did not finish among the prize winners. But a sort of self-hypnosis seemed to make it impossible for him to stop playing blindfold, and in 1905 he suffered a severe nervous breakdown. He was in a hospital for a while and recovered. But when he again gave blindfold performances he broke down once more, this time for good. He died in 1906, at the age of thirty-four.

The Cambridge Springs Tournament was won by Frank Marshall, who had gained his spurs in 1900 when he finished third in a great International Masters' Tournament at Paris, defeating Lasker and Pillsbury, the winners of first and second prizes, in the individual games he played with them. At Cambridge Springs Marshall finished fully two points ahead of Lasker. This remarkable victory had as a sequel an equally remarkable defeat. Marshall challenged Lasker to a match for the world championship, and Lasker beat him 8 to 0! This incident clearly illustrates the difference between match and tournament chess. In a tournament a player who wants to come out on top must avoid draws as much as possible, because a draw advances his score only half a point, while a dangerous competitor, winning his game of that round, would advance a full point. A somewhat risky style which puts the player himself as well as his opponent on more or less slippery ground, is therefore often more successful in tournament play than safe-and-sound strategy. In match play, on the other hand, there is no need to risk the loss of a game by going into unclear combinations. A draw advances the score of both contestants by the same amount.

Marshall always played risky chess; that is, he often embarked upon highly complicated attacks the end of which he could foresee just as little as his opponent. This made him very successful in tournaments, because fortune smiles on the attacking player much more frequently than on one who submits to laborious, time-taking defense. In match play Marshall was meat for such players as Emanuel Lasker, Tarrasch, or Capablanca, who were masters in quiet, positional play as well as in combinatory complications. Even I, who could not remotely compare with Marshall in tournament play, came close to defeating him in the match we played for the United States championship in 1923.

Both Marshall and Pillsbury were interesting examples of a strange mental phenomenon. They successfully concentrated all their faculties on chess, to the exclusion of every other intellectual interest. Trying to draw them into a conversation on any subject other than chess was a hopeless task. I have never seen anything like it, except possibly in opera stars or financial wizards.

Perhaps no match which Lasker played was looked forward to with greater general interest than the world championship contest with Tarrasch in 1908. Tarrasch was Lasker's senior by only seven years. Like Steinitz and Lasker, he was a chess thinker and had an academically trained mind. He practiced medicine most of his life, with the exception of the few weeks at a time which he took off to participate in chess tournaments—and the many hours every day which he spent in Munich's chess cafés. When he won four great international tournaments in a row, between 1889 and 1894, he was acknowledged to be Europe's leading master. His standing was confirmed by a tie match with the Russian giant, Tchigorin, who was generally considered to be the greatest player next to the world champion, Steinitz. The latter invited him to play a match for the title in Havana, but Tarrasch did not want to risk losing his medical practice by a prolonged absence from his office in Munich. Lasker also challenged Tarrasch to a match in the early nineties, but Tarrasch, who was not distinguished for his modesty, haughtily turned him down, suggesting that he first show his class in a number of first-rate tournaments.

He regretted this action very soon. After defeating Steinitz in 1894, Lasker finished ahead of Tarrasch in 1895 at Hastings, where Pillsbury won the first and Tchigorin the second prize. It was not until 1908 that Tarrasch—this time it was he who had to do the challenging—had the opportunity of measuring his strength in a match with Lasker.

The latter prepared for the match by a rest of three weeks in a woods near Berlin. All he did was walk and read. I can bear witness to the fact that he did not even take a chessboard with him. I went to visit him every day to play a game of Go with him, as he had asked me to do to while the time away. He never once mentioned the match, or the game of chess. The day before he left for Munich, where the match was to start, he made the first reference to it. He said: "If I should win the toss for the move, I think I will play the exchange variation of the Ruy Lopez. Can you tell me how anyone can lose that game?"

This question showed again how important the psychological moment was in Lasker's estimation. He did not want to lose the first game. He knew that a bad start always affected a player, no matter how great his self-confidence was. Lasker did draw the white pieces, played his variation, and won. When I greeted him in Düsseldorf, before the start of the second game, he gave me a knowing smile. The match ended in Lasker's favor, with a score of 8 wins, 3 losses, and 5 draws. He was the better fighter and the better psychologist of the two. Due to fine positional play, Tarrasch obtained a greatly superior game several times. But Lasker, knowing that clear positions were Tarrasch's forte, always found a way to complicate matters so as to make positional evaluations more difficult.

I mentioned that Tarrasch was a thinker. He had, besides, a methodical mind, and he was articulate. This made him an excellent teacher, and his books of annotated games are veritable treasure chests for the student of chess.

None of the other four masters whom I quoted as the outstanding European players of Lasker's day had Tarrasch's intellectual equipment. They were all men who had reached the top by dint of immense experience and, of course, the necessary dose of native gift. Maróczy was a tower of strength and solidity, Janovski a brilliant talent; but neither had the depth ever to reach Lasker's class. Besides, Maróczy was too gentle a person to develop the intensity and drive required to become a world champion. Janovski wasted most of his time at the roulette table, and he was too absurdly conceited to see his own short-comings. Only in a short match of four games did he succeed in equaling Lasker's score. In the other two matches which they contested, Lasker played with him like a cat with a mouse. The latter matches were played in Berlin in 1909 and 1910. The excuse which Janovski gave for his failure was characteristic of him. Instead of admitting that he spent his nights at roulette, he said to me one day: "I don't think I will win a game in this match. Lasker plays too stupidly for me to look at the board with any interest."

Lasker was in real danger of losing his title when, in 1910, he played a ten-game match with Schlechter. This was one of the most dramatic chess contests I have ever witnessed. Schlechter had been in the fore-front of tournament chess for several years, always finishing first or near the top, close to Tarrasch and Rubinstein. The latter had also challenged Lasker, pending his getting together the necessary purse, but Schlechter had found backers first.

Schlechter was a good-natured, kindly fellow, liked by everybody who knew him. It was hard to imagine him as world champion; for, like Maróczy, he seemed to lack the aggressive disposition one would expect in a challenger for a world title. His gentle manner of speech—even his unhurried way of walking—gave one the impression that he would much prefer sitting quietly in some beer garden, sipping a reasonable number of *Pilseners,* rather than battling an opponent on the chessboard for hours on end.

Schlechter usually rolled up more drawn games in a tournament than any other participant, and only the fact that he hardly ever lost a game made him land high up on most occasions. It was almost as if he did not have the heart to refuse a draw when an adversary asked him for it. In German a draw is called *Remis* (pronounced remee), a cor-ruption of the French *partie remise;* and a jokester had nicknamed Schlechter the "Master of the Vienna Remismonde." He lived up to this name in the match with Lasker; not that it ever came to the question whether or not he should accept a draw; he played so well that Lasker did not seem to be able to make any headway against him.

The first half of the match was played in Vienna. After Schlechter had drawn the first four games, Lasker finally obtained a winning advantage in the fifth game—only to lose through an unaccountable blunder in the end game. It must have been one of those cases of sudden *"Amaurosis Schacchistica,"* as Dr. Tarrasch had jokingly called the chess blindness which fatigue is apt to cause.

When the second half of the match started in Berlin, a feeling of drama pervaded the smoke-filled air of the huge ballroom in which over a thousand chess fans daily followed the moves of the match games on a large demonstration board. Lasker and Schlechter played in a smaller adjoining room reserved for chess patrons who could afford to buy ringside seats. Everyone realized that Lasker, for the first time in his career, was really fighting for his life. Schlechter drew one game after another, despite the fact that he did not by any means avoid complications. Somehow he proved himself equal to all problems which Lasker's strategy posed for him. After nine games the score was still 1 to 0 in Schlechter's favor, and when the tenth and last game was played, the excitement of the onlookers rose to the bursting point.

It seemed that both players were doing their best to make this the wildest battle of their life; Lasker, because he saw his only salvation in complications which might be too great for his antagonist to find a way out; Schlechter, because he probably disliked to win by the slim margin of one point. Whatever their reasons were, the game developed into the most exciting struggle in all chess history. The complexities of the combinations were such that analysis was altogether beyond the powers of the onlookers, and for more than an hour even the strongest players among them could not agree whether Lasker or Schlechter had the better of it. Finally, to the consternation of Lasker's friends, the complications he had produced turned in his disfavor. Schlechter reached a superior position which, at the very best, Lasker might have drawn. But the "equalizing injustice of chess" made Schlechter miss his way, as his opponent had done in the fifth game. He overlooked a hidden resource at Lasker's disposal, and what he had thought to be a winning combination was refuted and led to a losing end game. He resigned. The rest was pandemonium.

JOSÉ RAOUL CAPABLANCA, IDOL OF THE CHESS WORLD

The chess world had barely recovered from the excitement of this match when, in 1911, another sensational event threw it into fresh turmoil. The young Cuban, José Raoul Capablanca, who like Morphy, had learned the game from his father as a boy four years old, and who, again like Morphy, had won the championship of his home town at the age of twelve, had continued to parallel the career of the great American star. Upon appearing in New York when he was eighteen to enroll at Columbia University, he showed himself superior to the best American players in "lightning chess," a popular form of light game with a time limit of five or ten seconds per move. Within two years he had also proved better than the rest in serious chess, and in 1909 Frank Marshall accepted his challenge for a match. To the amazement of all, Capablanca won the match by 8 to 1 and fourteen draws. This victory over an international master induced the young Cuban to give up his engineering studies for good and to devote himself to a chess career.

When, two years later, a great International Masters' Tournament was organized in San Sebastián, Spain, the Cuban youngster asked for permission to participate. Against the protest of some of the masters, the tournament committee decided to make an exception in Capablanca's case and admit him, although he did not satisfy the condition which the organizers had stipulated, i.e., that every participant had to have a record of at least two third prizes in first-class masters' tournaments. Capablanca had had no opportunity as yet to play in a masters' tournament, but the result of his match with Marshall was considered sufficient evidence of his extraordinary strength.

With the exception of Lasker, every chess star of Europe was among the contenders. Capablanca put at rest all doubts which some of the masters still entertained as to his class. In the very first round he defeated Ossip Bernstein, next to Rubinstein Russia's strongest master. It was a brilliant game for which he received a special prize. Bernstein, knowing Marshall's style to be unsuited for match play, had thoroughly underestimated Capablanca's caliber even after his victory over Marshall. But he completely changed his opinion when he saw how the Cuban refuted his strategy in this first encounter of theirs, and told the other masters he would not be surprised to see the young fellow win the tournament. This is actually what happened. Although Rubinstein beat Capablanca in their individual game, the latter outnosed the Russian by a half point in the final score. The news of his victory was the sensation of the day, and it made the headlines of the newspapers throughout the world. That a novice, twenty-three years of age, should emerge ahead of all the world's leading chess stars in his first tournament was such a fantastic feat that it seemed explicable only by some entirely new strategic approach to the game which Capablanca might have found and which had not occurred to any of the other masters.

The pictures in the papers showed the Cuban to be a very handsome young man, and among the large audiences which he drew in every city he touched on a tour of simultaneous exhibitions shortly after the tournament, there was always an astonishing number of girls. The theory that the fair sex would never fancy the game of chess was obviously due for a revision.

I met Capablanca when he gave his exhibition in Berlin, and, like everybody else, was very much impressed with his personality. He was alert, well mannered, and despite a certain flair for showmanship which seems to be a natural characteristic of every champion, his obvious feeling of self-confidence was nicely tempered by that fundamental modesty which is one of the marks of real intelligence.

In his exhibitions he made perfectly staggering scores; and it was freely predicted that he would be the next world champion. Rubinstein was suddenly forgotten. The chess fans in general liked the idea of Capablanca holding the title, no doubt because they were able to identify themselves with him more readily than with the abstruse philosopher that was Emanuel Lasker.

Capablanca was as different as possible from Lasker in every way. Though gifted with a keen mind and well capable of abstract thought, he had no particular intellectual ambitions. His interests all lay in the field of competitive sports. He was a bridge expert, an excellent baseball player, and very good at tennis and billiards. The latter he played so well that whenever I saw him at it I could not help thinking of Disraeli's famous remark: "Young man, your prowess at this game bespeaks a wasted youth!"

There is no question that Capablanca spent a great deal of his life at play. But as one of the gods' favorites, who would begrudge him this? The Government of Cuba, which his fame had "put on the map," gave him a post in its Foreign Office. This relieved him of financial worry and enabled him to travel extensively. Thus the strong players of most countries had the opportunity of meeting him.

The year 1914 brought with it one of the great events in chess history: the first meeting between Capablanca and Lasker. Russian chess patrons had organized a most interesting International Masters' Tournament, with an entry list comprising eleven contenders drawn from three generations of chess players. Close to Capablanca's age were only two Russians, Aron Nimzovich, who was twenty-eight, and Alexander Alekhine, who was twenty-two. Both of them were destined to a place among the immortals of chess.

According to the conditions of the tournament, these eleven men played a preliminary round robin in St. Petersburg, and the five who attained the highest score were to play a final double round robin in Moscow.

Capablanca won the preliminary with 8 points, far ahead of Lasker and Tarrasch, who came next with 6½ points each, followed by Marshall and Alekhine, who made 6 points. This indicated such a superiority on Capablanca's part that his victory in the finals was a foregone conclusion, particularly since the scores made in the preliminary counted in the finals. Even a Lasker could not be expected to overcome a handicap of 1½ points in eight rounds when paired against the strongest players of the world.

Concerning the games he played with Lasker in Moscow, Capablanca once confided in me the following incident, which shows that his heart was in the right place. He felt, of course, quite certain he would win the first prize. He had the psychological advantage, in his two games with Lasker, that he could be satisfied with a draw, while Lasker was compelled to play for a win if he wanted to better or even equal Capablanca's score.

In the first game Lasker had the black pieces, and necessarily taking certain chances in his desire to avoid a draw at all costs, he suddenly found himself in a position in which he could not prevent the loss of two minor pieces for a Rook, which probably also meant the loss of the game.

Recalling that dramatic moment, Capablanca described how Lasker turned as white as a sheet when he realized his predicament, and how his hands trembled so violently he could hardly grasp the piece he wanted to move. Capablanca never doubted that before long he would be world champion. But, he said, he could not help a feeling of great pity welling up in his heart when he saw the paralyzing effect which the impending defeat had on the aging Lasker. He had held the chess scepter for twenty years, and no doubt realized at that moment that his time had come.

Lasker actually succeeded in drawing the ending, and in the second game he defeated Capablanca, pulling up to within half a point of him. Whether this was a bit too close even for the steel-nerved Cuban's comfort, or whether—as some news-writers claimed, and as Capablanca would not deny—the Russian girls proved too much of a distraction, Capablanca also lost the game which he played against the redoubtable Tarrasch the next day. This time it was Capablanca who deserved sympathy. Although he had run into a prepared opening variation, he had obtained a winning position, but then he made just one careless move and lost.

Lasker won the tournament with 13½ points, and Capablanca was second with 13, three full points ahead of Alekhine, who in turn finished 1½ points ahead of Tarrasch, thus becoming the youngest "grand master."

This result showed so clearly that Lasker and Capablanca were in a class by themselves that only a match between these two was of any interest as far as the world title was concerned.

World War I delayed the negotiations for the match, but in December 1920 conditions were finally agreed upon, and play started in March 1921. Twenty-four games were to be played, all at the chess club of Havana. Capablanca won, as almost everyone had expected, even though the contestants were unquestionably of equal class. But Lasker's age, and the privations he had had to go through during the war, were held to weigh heavily against him.

Capablanca's play was above criticism. Lasker was obviously not himself. He lost two good games through serious blunders, and in two more offered completely apathetic defense. He was unable to acclimate himself to the heat and bright sun of Havana, and resigned the match when the score was 4 to 0, with 10 draws. In his notes to the match, which he published in Germany, he praised Capablanca's game very highly, and while explaining his own inferior play as a result of the fatigue caused by the climate, he made it clear that he might have lost the match even if it had been contested in a climate to which he was accustomed. That the quality of his chess had not in the least deteriorated, and that his age had not yet noticeably affected his stamina, was indeed shown by the magnificent victories he won in the ten years which followed.

Capablanca went from triumph to triumph, and when he entered the New York Masters' Tournament of 1924, he could look back on a record that no one had equaled before him and probably no one ever will. He had played ninety-nine tournament and match games in ten years and had lost only one!

Any player who faced Capablanca in a serious game at that period was more or less resigned to meeting his inevitable fate. And when, in the fifth round of the tournament, Capablanca lost his game, there was indescribable excitement. The Cuban was paired with Richard Réti of Vienna, one of the great proponents of *modern chess,* and he had to defend himself against Réti's Opening, one of the many debuts hatched during the years following the war and even today considered one of White's strongest weapons.

Capablanca had had no opportunity as yet to play against this opening in the preceding rounds, but he seemed quite unconcerned. He conducted the game with that easy nonchalance and uncomplicated directness which had always distinguished his style and which had carried him to the high place of chess. After ten or twelve moves he not only obtained perfect equality but had even a shade the better of it.

Everyone was all the more dumfounded when, shortly before the end of the first session, the silence imposed on all spectators by large signs was pierced by someone shouting: "Capablanca resigned!" Unmindful of their clocks ticking away, all players rushed from their boards to learn what had happened. They found Capablanca and Réti at their table, both with unbelieving smiles. But it was true—Capablanca had miscalculated a maneuver through which he had thought to gain a Pawn, and he found himself left with an inferior position he could not hold. The world champion surrendered, and Réti was the hero of the day. The press carried the startling news to the far corners of the world, for Capablanca's name, known to every man in the street, was legendary already in his lifetime.

It seemed to take this shock to remind Cuba's chosen son of what the chess world expected of him. In the first four rounds, playing against Janovski, Emanuel Lasker, Alekhine, and myself, he had only managed to draw his games, so that after the fifth round he had but 2 out of 5 possible points, something which had not happened before in all the thirty-two years of his chess life. He showed what a great player he was, however, by rolling up 12½ points in the remaining fifteen rounds, finished 1½ points below Lasker, but 2½ points ahead of Alekhine.

Capablanca took Lasker's victory very good-naturedly. His standing had in no way suffered, for he had drawn one and won one of the two games he had played with him. I am sure he would have come closer to

Lasker's score if he had not shared the latter's strange views as to the roles that night and day are ordained to play in our lives. During the many years in which I saw a great deal of him, I do not remember his ever breakfasting before I had my lunch. The cause of his late evenings, however, was never mathematics or philosophy.

In tournaments Capablanca's habit of sleeping late sometimes got him into trouble. On one occasion—he was scheduled to play with me that day—he had not arrived in the play room at the time the game was supposed to begin, and the tournament director started his clock. Twenty, thirty, forty minutes went by, and still he did not appear. I became restive, for a player's game was forfeited when he was an hour late, and I did not want to win the game by default. After fifty minutes had elapsed I decided, against the tournament director's wishes, to try to locate Capablanca.

I telephoned him at his hotel, and he actually was still in his room. I said: "For heavens' sake, Capa, you must have overslept! If you don't get here within nine minutes, the tournament director is going to forfeit your game. Hurry over!"

He replied, very excitedly: "I just finished dressing, and I'll be there in time. You shouldn't have called me. This conversation made me lose a full minute!" And he hung up.

Naturally I was much upset by this ungracious reception of my well-meant reminder. But after Capablanca, rushing into the play room barely in time, had made his first fifteen moves with lightning speed and avoided overstepping his time, he regained his composure. He took my hand, and with his disarming laugh of a child he said: "It was nice of you to think of phoning me. But you certainly had me scared! You came awfully close to making me lose this game by default."

Under the strain of tournament pressure few chess masters have their nerves under sufficient control to avoid emotional flare-ups altogether. Capablanca was free from them, with extremely rare exceptions, of which the above-mentioned incident was one.

He successfully combined a gay temperament and adventurous playfulness with social grace and with the dignity befitting a world champion. His dignified bearing was entirely natural, never conscious, and it never affected his good sense of humor. When friends concocted pranks in which they needed his co-operation, he never refused, and when the joke was on him, he wholeheartedly entered into the general jollity.

Once an incident of this type, with a most amusing twist, occurred at a Hollywood beach club, where Capablanca happened to be as the guest of a friend. Some chess-playing members thought his visit was an excellent occasion to play a joke on Charles MacArthur, the playwright, who was a frequent visitor and who usually beat them at the game. They proposed to lure him into a game with the world champion, introducing the latter to him as a Mr. Joseph who "seemed to think he knew something about chess" and whom they would like to see shown up a bit. To make the plan more attractive to MacArthur, himself a practical jokester, they suggested that he allow himself to be introduced as Capablanca, the champion, duly scaring him from the start.

Everything worked according to plan, MacArthur walking into the trap with a gay smile of anticipation. But after only about ten or twelve moves had been made, a messenger brought a note to him from his wife, Helen Hayes, who had come into the room and, hearing about the joke, decided to take a hand in it. The note read: "Charlie, you are playing with Capablanca."

MacArthur, visibly startled for a short moment, quickly recovered and, with a grin, turned the tables on his friends. He got up and said: "I am awfully sorry, Helen wants me to drive her home right now and I must quit. Incidentally, Mr. Joseph is quite a fair player. I hope to have another opportunity of playing him soon. I am sure he can give me an interesting battle."

Capablanca, though always carrying himself with an air of absolute self-confidence, was free from all conceit. The impression he made on strangers is well illustrated by a story told me by Irving Chernev, the well-known chess author. Capablanca was to give an exhibition of simultaneous chess in New York, against some thirty opponents. The play room was packed with fans crowding around the players, who sat expectantly at their tables, waiting for the exhibition to start. One of the visitors asked Chernev, who was seated at one of the boards: "Would you kindly tell me which is Capablanca? I have never seen him." Chernev explained that he had not yet arrived. The other continued: "When he does, will you point him out to me?" Chernev smiled and said: "No, I won't have to. When Capablanca comes in, you will know he is the champion."

ALEXANDER ALEXANDROVICH ALEKHINE, LAST CHESS
ROMANTICIST

In 1927, in a match played at Buenos Aires, Capablanca lost his crown
to Alekhine. The match lasted several months, and the score was 6
wins, 3 losses, and 25 draws. No one believed that this result really indicated the relative strength of the two chess titans, and to this day
many experts think that Capablanca would have regained his title in a
return match. But the new champion saw to it that Capablanca never
got a second chance to compete with him.

Alekhine was unquestionably one of the greatest, if not *the* greatest,
inventive genius chess has had. There is hardly an opening variation
on which he has not, at one time or another, impressed the stamp of his
prodigious creativeness. If it is true that ceaseless hard work is one of
the attributes of genius, Alekhine certainly was an outstanding example. Every day he spent from four to eight hours at chess, analyzing
the games of other masters and trying to find improvements in the
openings used by them. Thus he presented a sharp contrast to Lasker
and Capablanca who, after reaching chess maturity, hardly ever spent
time on serious chess, except when they were engaged in match or
tournament play.

For chess fans who made the game their all-absorbing hobby, as well
as for masters who lived for chess alone, Alekhine was the ideal champion. They could understand him better than Emanuel Lasker, whose
intellectual interests were beyond their comprehension, and better than
Capablanca, whose lucid simplicity impressed them as eminently
practical but did not have an appeal comparable to the brilliance of
Alekhine's daring style.

Alekhine really loved chess. Whenever he discussed a game and
analyzed its ramifications, his eyes would light up and he would be
seized with a strange intensity, like a morphine addict.

He ate, slept, and dreamed chess. No matter what the theme of a
conversation, Alekhine would find an opportunity of modulating over
to the subject of chess.

Moreover, chess was his *only* love. I am sorry to say that in his
human relations he was governed by utter selfishness—even brutality.
He concealed these traits carefully when he felt that his career might

otherwise be adversely affected. I am recording these facts without personal animosity. During the many years of my close acquaintance with him we got along very well, and I learned of his bad character only much later.

A mutual acquaintance of ours, who had grown up with Alekhine in Moscow, and, like him, had fled from Russia during the revolution, revealed some of the depressing traits of Alekhine's character and explained them partly as the result of an unfortunate inheritance.

He came from an aristocratic but alcoholic family, and he grew up in an environment that could hardly be expected to produce an angel.

When the revolution broke out he served with the Intelligence Corps of the White Russian Army in Odessa. The Bolsheviks took the city, and he declared himself "liberated" and acted as spy for them. When the White Russians recaptured Odessa, Alekhine declared himself liberated again, and he volunteered for counterespionage. Finally the Bolsheviks prevailed, and Alekhine, not too sure that he had succeeded in destroying all damning evidence, summoned all his combinative powers to plot an escape.

Under compromising circumstances he practically coerced a young foreign woman to marry him. He thus secured permission to travel abroad. As soon as his train had crossed the Russian frontier, he deserted his wife—and their young son—crudely informing her that he had merely used her for the purpose of getting out of Russia.

Incidentally, this was the only *young* woman he ever married. All his subsequent wives—there were three of them—were at least twenty-five years older than he. Besides Bacchus, Oedipus must have been among his ancestry.

Alekhine learned chess as a child from his mother. In 1901, at the age of nine, he started to play blindfold, his ambition having been impelled in this direction by one of the extraordinary exhibitions of simultaneous blindfold play given by Pillsbury on his first European tour. He saw Pillsbury play sixteen games at a time in Moscow. Some thirty years later, at the Chicago World's Fair, Alekhine broke the world record in blindfold play by conducting thirty-two games simultaneously. I acted as umpire at that performance. It took ten hours, no longer than Morphy had taken to play eight games, and Pillsbury to play sixteen. But Alekhine did not play with the same unerring exactitude. He made a mistake every once in a while, correcting it only after I had repeated his move questioningly. Nevertheless, the performance was tremendously impressive. To my knowledge, it has been overshadowed since only by the Belgian, George Koltanovski, and the Pole, Mendel Najdorf. The latter, a resident of Buenos Aires, played forty games simultaneously, the performance lasting nearly twenty hours without interruption. How many of his opponents were vanquished by Najdorf's superior chess, and how many fell victims of sheer exhaustion, the report did not say.

In his early twenties, when Alekhine had reached complete chess maturity and, by winning a number of first-class master tournaments, had established his right to challenge Capablanca for the world title, the technique of the masters in general had reached such a degree of perfection, and openings had been analyzed so exhaustively, that almost the only field in which there was still room left for adventure was the middle game. Memory served sufficiently to get through the opening unhurt, and technique, more than anything else, was involved in the proper handling of most end games. The conduct of the middle game alone left the master a certain choice between various strategic possibilities. These were a matter of taste, and different players, according to their temperament, came to different decisions.

Both Capablanca's and Alekhine's conceptions on the chessboard were equal in depth. But Capablanca disliked complications and adventure. He preferred to know in advance where he was going. As Lasker said of him, his depth was that of a mathematician, not that of a poet. Alekhine, like Lasker, was a romantic, despite highly developed logical faculties. To him complications were never unwelcome. In fact, he always preferred them to a simple denouement. Again like Lasker, Alekhine realized that when pitted against an antagonist of equal class, correct psychological evaluation of the opponent gave a player a considerable advantage. He could hardly expect to secure an advantage through superior technique.

Thus, before his match with Capablanca, Alekhine studied the games of the latter most minutely, in order to arrive at the most promising psychological strategy; and his conclusions were correct. In none of the games of the match did he try to surprise Capablanca with a new opening variation. He knew the world champion would find a way to steer the opening into well-known paths. But in the middle game the challenger always chose the most complicated alternative that offered itself. He foresaw that in his desire for simplification Capablanca was apt to omit analyzing tactical possibilities in sufficient detail, thus laying himself open to a surprise attack.

Alekhine had never won a game from Capablanca, and it was perhaps natural that the latter would underestimate his strength. When the champion realized that this was what he had done, it was too late. Alekhine was already two points ahead and was satisfied to draw as long as Capablanca avoided unbalanced positions which offered opportunities to both sides.

None of the other masters of his day offered a serious threat to Alekhine's title, although he lost the championship temporarily, in 1935, to Dr. Max Euwe of Holland. He regained it in a return match two years later.

Alekhine's place among the immortals of chess is based not only on his successes against his competitors, but also on his work as chess author. For the advanced player, the game collections which Alekhine annotated are an endless source of instruction and enjoyment.

With the death of Alekhine in 1946, the chess world lost the last representative of its romantic period, which at the same time was the period most likely to produce great personalities. The scientific age in which we live has a tendency to turn the chess master more and more into a highly specialized technician, and individual experimenters with new ideas on the chessboard are under the same handicap as today's inventors, who can hardly hope for success unless their work forms part of the organized group efforts of research laboratories.

THE FOUNDERS OF MODERN CHESS

Among the masters who were contemporaries of Alekhine, there were two who, together with him, evolved entirely new conceptions concerning the strategy of the opening. They were Aron Nimzovich of St. Petersburg and Richard Réti of Vienna. Like Emanuel Lasker, both of these young chess stars were profound thinkers, highly educated, and distinguished from most of the other masters by their intense interest in the philosophical aspect of the game.

Réti was too much of a poet, not enough of a fighter, ever to offer a real threat to Capablanca's position as champion, although he defeated him in the game I referred to earlier. Nimzovich, however, might have become a second Lasker if he had not been handicapped by an almost pathological nervousness. I remember how in a masters' tournament at New York, which preceded the match between Alekhine and Capablanca, Nimzovich jumped up during a game and excitedly asked the tournament director to make a man leave the room who stood several feet away from the table at which Nimzovich's game was in progress. He could not endure an occasional jingling of keys in the spectator's pocket, which, to others, had not been audible at all.

In that tournament it looked for a while as if Nimzovich would finish in second place, ahead of Alekhine. Had he succeeded in doing so, Capablanca would have played him instead of Alekhine for the world title. But Nimzovich's nerves proved his undoing.

There was hardly a tournament in which he was not involved in some amusing controversy with fellow players. The funniest incident of this type occurred at a tournament in Hamburg, when Nimzovich was still a young university student. He had a strong aversion to another of the competing masters, who was also a student. His name was Walter John. Nimzovich provoked him in a rather childish manner by appearing almost a full hour late for the game with him, and blatantly exhibiting his feeling of superiority. He remained in his chair only a few seconds every time it was his turn to play and, between moves, instead of showing the slightest interest in the progress of the game, he lost himself in contemplation of the paintings on the walls of the play room, as if he had not seen them for hours every day of the two preceding weeks.

Early in the morning on the day following this game, Nimzovich was awakened by two gentlemen, dressed in formal morning coats, who introduced themselves as John's seconds and transmitted a challenge from him for a duel, leaving to Nimzovich the choice of weapons. At the same time, they gave him their cards and suggested that he send his own seconds to discuss matters with them.

Nimzovich told me the details of this interview with great relish at lunch. He had invited John's seconds, with exaggerated politeness, to stay for a cup of coffee, knowing full well that the code of German student fraternities which was involved in such matters (and which was no less childish than Nimzovich himself) would not permit them to accept his hospitality. When they turned to leave, he had expressed his regrets that he knew of no one in Hamburg on whom he could impose to act as his second, but he had assured them that he was prepared to fight the duel anyway. However, he had added with a grin, he would use fists as weapons, and, rolling up his sleeves and exhibiting his bulging muscles, he had counseled them to dissuade John from his plan, as there would probably be very little left of him at the conclusion of the fight. The seconds took leave with an expression of haughty contempt, and the duel never took place.

A certain aggressive criticism of anyone dissenting from his opinions runs like a red thread throughout Nimzovich's writings. All the same, his books contain a wealth of information indispensable to the aspirant to mastership. He swept from the shelves of the student the strategic theories which two generations of chess players had accepted as gospel. The master who, more than anyone else, had preached that gospel, and who naturally came in for most of Nimzovich's criticism, was Tarrasch. In the controversy which developed, Tarrasch was classically disdainful of his antagonist's subversive doctrine, but he was also twenty-five years older, and therefore could no longer successfully argue the matter with Nimzovich over the chessboard. The latter's ideas, however, were destined anyway to prove their superiority. They were amplified by the work of Réti and Alekhine, and crystallized into the modern style of play.

The essence of this style was distilled from a profound insight into the exigencies of "center control." On the first move the older masters had almost always advanced one of the two center Pawns as a matter of course. The players of the new school questioned the very foundations of established chess strategy, just as the founders of modern science had questioned our fundamental concepts of time and mass. The conclusions reached by the new school seemed heresy, but they gradually proved their validity. The second player, they argued, by advancing his center Pawn on the first move, offered White a welcome target to shoot at; and only by first preparing the occupation of the center with other moves could Black hope to maintain a hold on it. Some enthusiastic young supporters of Nimzovich's theory questioned the wisdom of starting the game with the customary double step of the King's Pawn even when playing White. One of them, the highly gifted Hungarian Julius Breyer, coined a chess epigram when he said that with the immediate advance of his King's Pawn, White took the first step toward digging his own grave.

It was characteristic of modern chess to lure the opponent's center Pawns forward and to beleaguer them with Bishops placed in the long diagonals. To get the Bishops so posted, an additional Pawn move was required. This was something abhorrent to the chess classicist who insisted that in the opening stage of the game Pawns should be moved only when absolutely necessary to open a path to the battlefield for an immobile piece. But the young masters proved time and again that the loss of a move entailed in the fianchetto development of the Bishop was often more than offset by the greater influence of that Bishop on the center of the board.

These ideas of the modern school are lucidly expounded in two books: Nimzovich's *My System* and Réti's *The New Ideas in the Game of Chess*. Another original contribution to the subject is *Die Hypermoderne Schachpartie,* by the scintillating wit and brilliant player Dr. Savielly Tartakover, an Austrian master who became a French citizen. At the same time a contemporary and an epigone of Nimzovich, Alekhine, and Réti, and more than twice the age of most masters who opposed him after World War II, he wielded a keen-edged sword until his death in 1956, ever impressively propagating the teachings of the great triumvirate of modern chess.

Another master who for years actively collaborated with the founders of the new school was the Russian Efim Bogolyubov (meaning God's beloved), a naturalized German. He never was an articulate of modern chess, but confined himself to a more practical demonstration of its superiority by winning one tournament after another. His greatest triumph was his victory in the great Moscow tournament of 1925, in which he far outdistanced Lasker and Capablanca. But his daring style was less suited for match play. Alekhine defended his world title against him successfully without much difficulty.

I had exciting battles with both Tartakover and Bogolyubov in their heyday, and it warmed my heart to see them hard at it until they died, ever embroiled in tournaments, their fighting spirit undaunted. With "one eye gay, the other moist," I recall a remark which Tartakover made to me in Hamburg just forty years ago, after a round in which Oldrich Duras of Prague had beaten him. He said: "The great Oldrich served me with a new variation, which gave me indigestion. But next year's new world champion is going to refute that variation and eat Duras alive."—"Who do you think will be the next world champion?" I asked him in surprise.—"Well, I naturally!" he replied, an inimitable mixture of bravado, irony, and hopelessness in his voice.

Poor Tartakover! He never got there, and no doubt he realized instinctively he never would. With all his intelligence, culture, knowledge, and ability to work hard, he lacked a most important quality which his fellow-aspirant Alekhine had in abundance: a furious drive, a devastating ambition, blotting out all other desires until the goal is reached.

FOURTEEN-YEAR-OLD "MOZART OF CHESS"*

by Harold C. Schonberg

In a few weeks the winner of the United States Chess Championship, the United States Open Chess Tournament, the United States Junior Championship, and several other assorted baubles will go to the hospital and have his adenoids out, thus missing a few days at Erasmus Hall High School in Brooklyn, where he is a sophomore. Bobby Fischer, who will be fifteen on March 12, [1958] has been taking on all comers in chess ever since he wandered into the Manhattan Chess Club at the age of twelve and proceeded to startle the *potzers* with his phenomenal ability at "rapid transit." A *potzer*, otherwise known as a wood-pusher, is a species of chess player who ranks about Class Z in a stern hierarchy that (in the American ratings system) starts with Class B and works up through Class A, Expert, Master, Senior Master and Grand Master. Rapid transit is ten-second chess, in which the good player intuitively feels rather than studies positions, since he has only ten seconds to make each move. "Bobby was a demon at rapid transit," one of the masters at the Manhattan Chess Club says. "We would gather around to watch him. Skill at rapid chess is always a sign of innate talent, the best there is."

Bobby hung around the club for a year or so, sharpening his game in competition with some of the best players in America. Then he took off with everything in sight, including the American championship in January. Normally reserved and skeptical chess critics find no words to describe Bobby Fischer accurately. He has been called a miracle, the Mozart of chess, the greatest natural genius the game has ever known and a shoo-in for the world's championship if he progresses as he has in the past two years. "Never before in all chess history has there been such a phenomenon," says Hans Kmoch, formerly a renowned player, author of recondite chess treatises and secretary of the Manhattan Chess Club. "At his age, neither Morphy, nor Capablanca, nor Reshevsky had such achievements. In his last three tournaments, Bobby won without losing a game and he drew very few."

Bobby became United States champion on Jan. 7. He turned up at the Manhattan Chess Club that night wearing dungarees and a T shirt. (He has never been known to wear a necktie and only a short time ago his mother finally managed to get him out of sneakers and into shoes.) He was a half point ahead, going into the final game, and he drew his match with Abe Turner in short order. That left Samuel Reshevsky, in second place, a full point behind. Reshevsky, one of the most dangerous players alive, had to win to tie Bobby for the championship.

Having nothing much to do, pending the outcome of Reshevsky's game with William Lombardy, Bobby wandered off to a corner of the club and began to play blitz with some friends. (Blitz is quicker than ten-second chess—ten seconds per move quicker.) In the meantime, a crowd gathered around the Reshevsky–Lombardy game. Reports and rumors were relayed to Bobby, who was trying to appear nonchalant. Finally, he could stand it no longer, and he elbowed his way through the crowd. He glanced at the board and came back. "Gee," he said, "Lombardy's playing like a *house!*"

A half hour later, Bobby stopped blitzing and walked over to take another look at the game. This time, he took a really long look, about fifteen seconds or so. "Reshevsky's busted," he announced, returning. "Lombardy's got his rooks doubled on the knight file. What an attack he's got!" All the *potzers* in the vicinity set up the position and tried to determine how the great Reshevsky was busted. "Hey, Fischer," one of them called out, "how's Sammy going to lose? We figure a draw." Fischer came over, bored. "Bill plays here," he said. "Reshevsky plays here; he must, because if he doesn't . . ." and then followed a fast analysis of the position. "I give Reshevsky ten more moves," Bobby concluded, "and then he must resign."

Within ten moves, Reshevsky resigned and a great yell went up. Bobby started to jump around and dance, and then congratulated Lombardy, a saturnine, heavy-set boy of twenty who is the world junior champion and a student at City College. "You played tremendously," Bobby said. "Well, what else could I do?" grinned Lombardy. "You forced me to beat Sammy."

As a result of his victory, Bobby is entitled to play this August in the interzonal tournament in Yugoslavia. The high-ranking scorers there will then meet in a challenger's tournament and the winner will play Vassily Smyslov, the Russian who is current titleholder, for the world championship. Admirers of Bobby worry about the showing he will make in the interzonal, for he has never before met players of this caliber. But they also worried before the United States tournament. Arthur Bisguier, whom Bobby dethroned as American champion, wrote in the *Chess Review*:

"Bobby Fischer, our youngest luminary, should finish slightly over the center mark. He is probably the player in the tournament with the greatest familiarity with the latest wrinkles in opening theory. . . . Still, he has had no experience in tournaments of such consistently even strength. Neither he nor his admirers should be discouraged if his result here does not quite measure up to his other triumphs. This is a strong field."

Bobby learned the moves at the age of six, shortly after he had come to New York to live. He was born in Chicago, in 1943, after which his family started a restless traipse that took them to Oregon, Arizona, and California. His parents were divorced in 1945, and his mother took all kinds of jobs to keep the family going. When the three of them—Mrs. Fischer, Bobby, and his sister Joan—came to New York in 1948, Mrs. Fischer studied nursing. She is now a registered nurse completing courses for an A.M. in nursing education at New York University.

Joan, now twenty, and also a registered nurse, who has just entered pre-medical school, taught Bobby the moves. They got a chess set and puzzled out from the directions what to put where. Games were what Bobby loved. Mrs. Fischer says that as a baby he was intensely interested in puzzles. "He would get those Japanese interlocking rings, and things like that, and take things apart I couldn't figure out at all." Bobby liked chess but it didn't seem to make much impact on him.

In the meantime he was proving a problem in public school. Fresh from California, he had never worn a shirt, and he rebelled against the necessity of dressing up. In the fourth grade, the Brooklyn Community–Woodward school gave him a scholarship. The boy's intelligence quotient has never been made public, but school authorities indicate that it is high in the upper percentile. "Brooklyn Community did a lot for Bobby," says Mrs. Fischer.

Bobby's chess playing was encouraged by Brooklyn Community. Teachers there remember him running around with copies of *Schachmaty* (the Russian chess publication) stuffed into his pocket.

He was an average student and something of a nonconformist. "We kept him as happy as possible while he was here," an official of the school says. "We were able to adjust to him." It was noticed that Bobby was not particularly interested in the academic life, but that he showed tremendous and fierce concentration on winning in competitive sports.

"He incited a great deal of interest in chess here," says one of his teachers. "He easily beat everybody, including the chess-playing members of the faculty. No matter what he played, whether it was baseball in the yard, or tennis, he *had* to come out ahead of everybody. If he had been born next to a swimming pool he would have been a swimming champion. It just turned out to be chess." Bobby hates to lose. Two or three years back, he would, if he dropped a game, retire to a corner and cry. He no longer cries, but he still feels terrible when he loses.

At the age of eight or so, Bobby started going to the Brooklyn Chess Club, where Carmine Nigro, its president, took an interest in the child. "He helped me more than anybody," says Bobby. While most children of his age were reading comic books and reluctantly doing homework, Bobby was subscribing to the aforementioned *Schachmaty* and all of the American chess magazines. Naturally his homework took second place. At Erasmus Hall he is described as an average student, "very good in some subjects, not so good in others, but a very bright boy."

When he first came to the Manhattan Chess Club he was short and cherubic-looking. Suddenly he started growing. He is now 5 feet 10 inches tall and weighs about 140 pounds. He is at an awkward emotional age. He likes being a celebrity but has not acquired the social graces to handle his new position easily. Usually he is shy and introverted; at other times, boisterous. Only among chess players does he really feel at home; then he is relaxed and happy. "Don't forget," says an admirer of his, "that he's really a child thrown into a man's world. He's a nice kid. He may be a little cocky, and why shouldn't he be? Right now when he's away from the chess world he has a tendency to go into a shell. He'll get over it."

A growing boy, Bobby has a growing boy's appetite. He is well-built and may make a fine athlete. When he won the championship, he was invited to Grossinger's. Tony Kastner, the ski pro there, found Bobby was following him around. "Bobby will make a good skier," Kastner says. "His co-ordination is terrific." In return for ski lessons, Bobby gave Kastner chess lessons.

He is an abnormally sensitive and touchy boy who is only just beginning to realize that there is a world outside of kings, queens, rooks, and pawns. Over the chessboard in tournament play, he is quiet, assured, and completely mature, though his fingernails are bitten to the quick. In offhand chess games such as blitz, he carries on a rapid, good-natured, nervous patter in a voice that has not settled down as yet. "You dare do this to *me*? C'mon, make a move. . . . Ouch! . . . Look at *him*! You're busted and you don't know it. Resign, weakie, resign!" Outside of the chess world he seems to have few friends. Often when speaking with adults he does not know well, he adopts an air of sullen bravado.

As yet, Bobby has no plans for the future. He doesn't know if he wants to go to college. "If I had a lot of money I'd like to play in chess tournaments. But you can't make a living in chess." (His prize for the American championship was $600.) He does know one thing: he doesn't like newspaper men and says so. He feels that he has always been misquoted or made out to be a freak.

"Those guys always write bad about me," he says. "They say I'm stupid, that I have nothing but a talent for chess. It's not true. I'm good in some sports. I'm not saying I'm terrific, but I played some tennis, did some iceskating, and used to be good at baseball. That was when I was young, years ago. We played stickball in the street. I'm pretty good in Spanish, and I like science, astronomy most of all."

He says that these days he doesn't study chess much, a remark that causes great amusement and some disbelief at the Manhattan Chess Club. "Last year, I concentrated on end-game positions for a few months. Now I'm playing through end games and tournament books." He has a tremendous knowledge of "book chess," that is, nearly a total recall of all standard openings and the various lines thereof. He doesn't look for new moves, contenting himself with taking advantage of a positional weakness in an opponent. "It's getting harder and harder to find new moves," says Bobby. "The Russians do, though. They've got 50,000 people analyzing opening theory."

If memorization were all that was needed to make a great player, the woods would be full of them. What makes a great player? "Practice. Study. Talent," is Bobby's answer. A strong element of imagination and even creation enters into chess on its highest level; and each great player is a stylist. Morphy was a romantic; Réti a hypermodern; Capablanca a classicist. An expert in chess can distinguish an Alekhine game as easily as an expert in art can identify an unsigned Guardi or Pissarro.

One American chess master describes Bobby's style as "effortless. Reminiscent of Capablanca. He's hardly ever in time pressure." (In most American tournaments, the player must complete forty moves in two hours—two and a half hours, in championship tournaments—and in complicated positions a player may find himself with only two minutes to make fifteen moves.)

"He has a beautiful classical style," says the same master, "and practically no idiosyncrasies. He doesn't favor, say, two bishops or a certain type of position. I see no perceptible weakness in any part of his game, and as a tactician he's marvelous." The late Dr. Savielly T. Tartakover, one of the great players, once defined tactics as "knowing what to do when there is something to do; strategy is knowing what to do when there is nothing to do."

Bobby's youth helps. Chess is a young man's game. In all history, there has not been a great chess player who failed to make his mark before he was 20. In the late teens and early twenties, the mind can absorb more and react more quickly, while the body can stand up under the rigors of heavy tournament play: five hours daily, for two weeks or more, during which the brain bubbles and every atom of one's intellectual being is concentrated outside time and space on the infinite possibilities of chess pieces in combination; nights of analysis; a restless turning in bed while games are mentally played over and new tactics devised. Players have been known to lose five pounds during a tournament.

Most chess players fade away after the age of forty-five. They make mistakes they never previously have made, they don't handle themselves well under time pressure, and new theory passes them by. Along comes a kid who is up on the latest analyses from all over the world and the older man is literally beaten in the opening few moves, though he may struggle for forty or so.

Dr. Kmoch still sputters when he recalls the night Bobby won the championship. "In no other country in the world," he says, "is it conceivable that there would be not one word from the Government. It's inconceivable, fantastic. The entire chess world is stunned with amazement by the announcement that a fourteen-year-old boy has won the American championship—and silence from the authorities."

Kmoch thinks that Bobby is at least one answer to the sputnik, for chess is the Russian national sport. He and many others in the chess world have been reading with interest about the cultural interchange plan arranged by former Soviet Ambassador Georgi N. Zaroubin and William S. B. Lacy, special assistant to the Secretary of State on East–West exchanges. Under the terms of the agreement, some five hundred Americans will visit the Soviet Union next year. The betting in the Manhattan Chess Club is a queen against a pawn that no chess players will be represented.

"Bobby may not have the funds to compete this August in Yugoslavia," Kmoch says indignantly. "Possibly some of the wealthier players in the club will raise the money. And possibly they may not. Should it be their responsibility?"

But it probably will be private funds that will take care of the trip. "We'll have to do something for him," says Maurice J. Kasper, president of the Manhattan Chess Club and treasurer of the American Chess Foundation. Neither the A.C.F. nor the United States Chess Federation, however, has much money. Last year the United States was not represented in the Chess Olympiad. Forty countries sent teams, but the United States players could not raise enough money.

Invitations for Bobby to play in tournaments or to give exhibitions have been pouring in from all over the world. Canada wants him. Mar del Plata in Argentina, where an important tournament is often held, has extended an invitation. England would like to see him in the Hastings tournament. Russia not only has invited him but has promised to pick up the tab for his entire visit there.

Bobby primarily wants to go to Yugoslavia, for from there lies the road to the world championship. He is cagy about his chances in that assemblage. "Let's see who's in it," he says. "I won't predict. All I have to do is end up in the upper half of the tournament. That qualifies me for the challenger's tournament." Bobby leaves little doubt about his confidence of getting in the upper half. He was reminded that the best players of the four leading chess nations—Russia, Yugoslavia, Czechoslovakia, and Argentina—would be represented. He shrugged his shoulders. "They're good too," he said.

*"Of course, I remember what day it is. It was nine years ago
today I checkmated Reinfeld in 12 moves."*

End Game Studies

Here is a miniature world hidden away from the general gaze, a world passed by as far as most chess players are concerned. But it is also a world of inexhaustible charm, delightful surprises, incredible resources—a world where the unreal is made real and where, to paraphrase Dylan Thomas, defeat has no dominion.

And the pity of it all is that so few players are aware of these enchanting studies. I make bold to say that you may find them even more engrossing than actual games, for these endings have been worked and reworked lovingly by master craftsmen who may take years to achieve one perfect ending. Not worth it, you say? Sample these studies and you will change your mind.

A far cry it is from the first simple ending credited to an Arabian writer of four centuries ago to the unbelievably subtle and impish masterpiece that concludes the section. Yet in the last analysis our wonderment centers on this one thought: how is it possible to concentrate so much beauty into so little space and time?

(See Diagram 1 on page 58)

With a whole Rook to the good, White ought to have an easy win. But one of his Rooks is attacked, and worse yet, Black threatens . . . R–R1 mate. White neatly solves both difficulties with:

    1   R–KR5!   RxR

Forced, as White was also threatening 2 R–QR6 mate.

    2   R–R6ch   K moves

    3   R–R5ch and wins

The confiscation of Black's Rook was admirably engineered.

FIRDUSI (about 1500)

BLACK

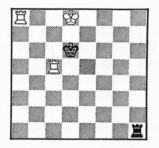

WHITE

1. White to play and win

B. HORWITZ and J. KLING, 1851

BLACK

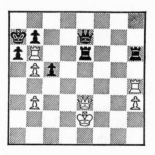

WHITE

2. White to play and win

(See Diagram 2 on page 58)

This old-fashioned problem is naïve, brutal if you will. Yet the solution is appealing.

The question is, how does White survive the terrible pin on his Queen?

   1 R/N6xR   RxR

White's predicament seems in no way improved.

   2 P–N6ch!   KxP

What else? If the King goes to the last rank, White forces mate with 3 R–R8ch etc.

   3 R–R6! and wins

The counter-pin saves White's Queen and decides in his favor.

H. RINCK, 1915

BLACK

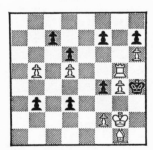

WHITE

3. White to play and draw

Though White is a Rook and Bishop ahead, he has no way of stopping the Black Queen Knight Pawn and Queen Pawn. And yet he has a way of avoiding defeat.

   1 P–N6!   PxP

Black *must* take, for example 1 . . . P–N7?; 2 PxP, P–N8/Q; 3 P–B8/Q, KxR; 4 Q–KB5ch, KxP; 5 Q–B6 mate.

   2 R–R5ch   KxP
   3 R–R1!   . . . .

If Black advances either of his foremost Pawns, White wins with P–B3ch followed by a Bishop move.

3	....	P–B6ch
4	K–R2	....

On 4 . . . K–R5 or a Pawn move, White is stalemated! Now we see the point of P–N6! White had to get rid of this Pawn in order to make the stalemate possible. (If Black releases the stalemate on move 4 with some such move as 4 . . . K–B5, White replies 5 K–R3 followed by 6 B–R2 and is then ready to win the advanced Black Pawns.)

K. KNOTHE, 1959

BLACK

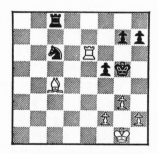

WHITE

4. White to play and win

The naturalness of the setting is quite remarkable.

1	P–B4ch	K–N5

If 1 . . . K–R4; 2 B–K2 mate.

2	K–N2	....

White threatens 3 B–K2 mate.

2	....	N–Q5
3	R–KR6!!	....

White threatens 4 P–R3 mate.

3	....	PxR
4	P–R3ch	K–R4

5   B–B7 mate

Black's King is hemmed in by his own Pawn.

P. HEUAECKER

BLACK

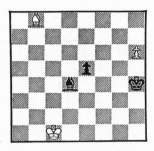

WHITE

5. White to play and win

The stark simplicity of the position argues the impossibility of a win: if White advances his Pawn, Black replies 1 . . . P–K5 and the ending is clearly drawn.

And yet the win is there:

       1   B–R7!   . . . .

For if 1 . . . BxB?; 2 P–R7 and White's Pawn queens.

       1   . . . .   B–R8

       2   K–N1   B–B6

       3   K–B2   B–R8

It is not clear that White has gained anything, but his next move is certainly startling.

       4   B–Q4!!   BxB

First point: if 4 . . . PxB; 5 K–Q3 and the advance of White's Pawn cannot be stopped.

       5   K–Q3!   . . . .

Second point: Black cannot play . . . P–K5ch while his Bishop is exposed to capture. Therefore he must move his Bishop.

<table>
<tr><td>5 . . . .</td><td>B–N7</td></tr>
<tr><td>6 K–K4!</td><td>. . . .</td></tr>
</table>

Third point: Black's Pawn is blockaded and his Bishop is shut off. The White Pawn now queens by force!

F. AMELUNG

BLACK

WHITE

6. White to play and win

Despite White's enormous material advantage it requires some very delicate maneuvering to take the sting out of Black's threatened Pawn promotion.

<table>
<tr><td>1 B–K2ch!</td><td>K–Q7</td></tr>
</table>

If Black captures the Bishop, 2 RxPch solves White's problem at once. Or if 1 . . . K–B8; 2 B–Q3 and again the Pawn falls.

<table>
<tr><td>2 K–R3!</td><td>K–B6</td></tr>
</table>

Here 2 . . . K–B8; 3 R–N3 leads to the main line of play.

<table>
<tr><td>3 R–N3ch</td><td>K–Q7</td></tr>
<tr><td>4 R–Q3ch!</td><td>KxB</td></tr>
</table>

Or 4 . . . K–B8; 5 R–QB3!, K–Q7; 6 K–N2 and White wins.

<table>
<tr><td>5 R–QB3</td><td>K–Q7</td></tr>
<tr><td>6 K–N2</td><td>. . . .</td></tr>
</table>

White now captures the Pawn, winning.

Very pretty play, but 2 K–N3 seems much simpler.

S. KRENZITZKY, 1921

BLACK

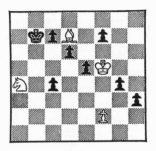

WHITE

7. White to play and draw

To all appearances White's pieces are singularly ill-placed to stop Black's menacing Rook Pawn. But if you follow the composer's thought, you will see that White's desperate-looking situation is really ideal for the purpose.

      1 N–B5ch!   PxN

On King moves White has 2 N–K4 followed by N–N3, squelching the Rook Pawn's queening ambitions.

      2 KxKP!   P–R7

"So what," says Black.

      3 BxP!   P–R8/Q
      4 B–B3ch!   QxB
         Drawn

White is stalemated! Very neat.

(*See Diagram 8 on page 64*)

A tricky position. "Obviously" White can win easily with a Bishop check followed by RxP. Actually it is not so obvious, for example 1 B–B6ch?, K–Q3!; 2 RxP, P–K8/Q; 3 RxQ and Black is stalemated. So White must find a different way:

      1 B–B5ch   K–Q1

After 1 . . . K–Q3; 2 RxP it is all over, as there is **no stalemate.**

R. RETI, 1928

BLACK

WHITE

8. *White to play and win*

  2 B–Q3!   . . . .
But not 2 RxP?, P–K8/Q; 3 RxQ and again Black is stalemated.
    2 . . . .   P–K8/Q
    3 B–N5! and wins

Black has to give up his Queen (. . . Q–R4ch) in order to stop
R–K8 mate.

Curiously enough White has an alternative winning method in
2 B–Q7!, P–K8/Q (or 2 . . . KxB; 3 RxP and White wins); 3 B–N5!
with the same position as above.

(*See Diagram 10 on page 65*)

End-game literature abounds in hopeless-looking situations in which
White avoids coming to grief because of a Black Pawn that cannot
be stopped from queening. But this is surely the most hopeless-looking
of them all.

    1 P–R7   K–N2
    2 N–B7!   KxP
Otherwise White's Pawn queens.
    3 N–N5ch!!   PxNch
Otherwise the Knight retreats to Rook 3 or Bishop 3.

F. SCHOUTEN, 1926

BLACK

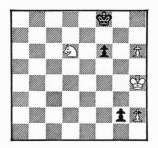

WHITE

9. White to play and draw

4 K–R3!   Drawn

If Black promotes to a Queen or Rook, White is stalemated. If Black promotes to a Bishop or Knight, White removes the remaining Black Pawn with 5 K–N4 and (if need be) 6 P–R4. All very sharp and clear.

(*See Diagram 10 on page 66*)

Despite White's huge material advantage the situation looks hopeless for him, as the Black Pawns look unstoppable. For example, 1 B–B1 is answered by 1 . . . P–N7. However:

1 B–B1!   P–N7

Naturally 1 . . . P–R7 would not do because of 2 B–N2, P–R8/Q; 3 BxQ, P–N7; 4 B–Q6ch! or 4 B–N6ch (4 BxP?? stalemates Black!) followed by BxP and wins.

2 BxP   PxB

What now?

3 B–N8!!   . . . .

For if 3 . . . P–N8/Q; 4 B–R7ch winning the new Queen.

3 . . . .   K–N3

And now White seems to have exhausted his resources.

4 B–K5!   P–N8/Q

H. RINCK, 1917

BLACK

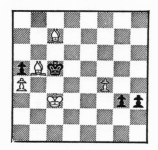

WHITE

10. White to play and win

    5   B–Q4ch and wins

After 5 . . . QxBch; 6 KxQ the King and Pawn ending is easily won for White. The composer of this one obviously had a sense of humor.

(See Diagram 11 on page 67)

Clever Rook maneuvers give White a beautiful win.

    1   R–QR1!   . . . .

Necessary in order to deflect Black's Rook from the second rank.

    1   . . . .   RxR
    2   R–KR4   N–B2

White was threatening 3 R–R8ch followed by mate.

    3   R–R8ch!   NxR
    4   PxP and wins

Black's helplessness is touching. White is threatening 5 PxN/Qch (or 5 PxN/Rch) followed by mate. If Black plays 4 . . . N–B2 he allows 5 P–N8/Qch or /Rch forcing mate next move.

P. FARAGO, 1935

BLACK

11. White to play and win

J. BEHTING, 1889

BLACK

WHITE

12. White to play and win

(See Diagram 12 on page 67)

This ingenious study is fairly easy. The nicely co-ordinated activity of the White pieces makes a very pleasing impression.

1	B–QB5ch!	K–Q1

On 1 . . . QxB the winning line is 2 P–Q8/Qch, KxQ; 3 N–K6ch followed by 4 NxQ. White will win all the Black Pawns and then force checkmate with his Bishop and Knight.

2	N–K6ch	KxP
3	B–K8ch!	KxB
4	N–B7ch	. . . .

White continues 5 NxQ winning.

R. BIANCHETTI, 1925

BLACK

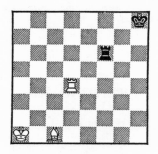

WHITE

13. White to play and win

Repeatedly we have to marvel at the rich effects composers obtain from what appear to be hopelessly barren settings. This ending is probably the most resourceful of the whole selection.

1	B–N2!!	. . . .

With two pieces masking the long diagonal, Black is forced to lose his Rook no matter how he plays.

Thus, 1 . . . K–N1 allows 2 R–KN4ch, while 1 . . . K–R2 allows 2 R–KR4ch or 2 R–Q7ch.

1 . . . K–N2 loses to 2 R–KB4 or 2 R–Q6. What about Rook moves?

In the event of 1 . . . R–QR3ch or 1 . . . R–B8ch, White interposes his Rook, giving a cross-check which wins at once. Most other Rook moves lose the Rook, but note that on 1 . . . R–KN3 White has 2 R–Q8 dbl ch, K–R2; 3 R–KR8 mate, while on 1 . . . R–B2 we get 2 R–KR4 dbl ch, K–N1; 3 R–R8 mate.

The longest resistance arises from: 1 . . . R–B1 or 1 . . . R–KR3. Here is what happens:

1	. . . .	R–KR3
2	R–KN4 dis ch	K–R2
3	R–N7ch	K–R1
4	K–N1!! and wins

And now, wherever Black moves his Rook, it is lost by discovered check. However, if 4 . . . R–KB3 White must not play 5 BxR?? because of stalemate. Any Rook move (except R–KR7 dbl ch, or R–N8 dbl ch) will win handily for him.

Similarly, if 1 . . . R–B1; 2 R–Q7 dis ch, K–N1; 3 R–KN7ch, K–R1; 4 K–R2!! and White wins in analogous fashion.

A wonderfully rewarding study.

K. A. L. KUBBEL, 1909

BLACK

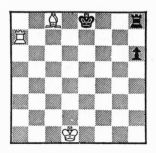

WHITE

14. White to play and win

(See Diagram 14 on page 69)

White's astonishing simplicity of means crushes Black with remarkable economy of effort.

         1   B–B5!   R–B1

White was threatening to win Black's Rook with 2 R–R8ch.

Note that 1 . . . R–N1 is foiled by 2 R–R8ch, K–B2; 3 B–K6ch! etc.
Or 1 . . . K–B1; 2 B–R7!, P–R4; 3 K–K1, P–R5; 4 K–B1, P–R6;
4 K–N1 and Black must play . . . K–K1 allowing R–R8ch winning Black's Rook.

         2   B–N6ch   K–Q1
         3   B–B7!   P–R4

Neither King nor Rook can move.

         4   K–K1   P–R5
         5   K–B1   P–R6
         6   K–N1   P–R7ch

Black hopes for 7 KxP, R–R1ch followed by the departure of Black's Rook from the first rank.

         7   K–R1! and wins

Black must lose his Rook. A very rewarding study.

F. SACKMANN, 1919

BLACK

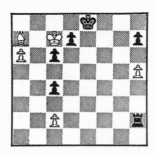

WHITE

15. White to play and win

The function of the Bishop is to trip up the Rook in its effort to prevent the Pawn from queening. But 1 B–N6, RxBP; 2 P–R7, R–QR7; 3 K–N7, P–B6 is not the way. Instead:

      1   B–B2!   . . . .

For if 1 . . . RxB; 2 P–R7 and the Pawn queens. Note also that 1 . . . R–R8 loses to 2 B–Q4, while 2 . . . R–R6 is refuted by 3 B–B5 etc.

      1 . . . .   RxP

Black hopes to play . . . R–R4.

      2   B–N6   R–R6

Now Black wants to play . . . R–R6.

      3   B–B5   R–R8

Maybe White will let him play 4 . . . R–R8.

      4   B–Q4   R–R6
      5   B–N2!   . . . .

Here the Bishop performs a double function, preventing the Rook from reaching Queen Rook 6 or Queen Rook 8.

      5 . . . .   R–R4

Still praying to get the Rook to QR4.

      6   B–B3 and wins

For if 6 . . . R–R6 or R–R8; 7 P–R7 wins for White.

H. WEENINK, 1917

BLACK

WHITE

16. White to play and win

(See Diagram 16 on page 71)

White's Pawn is an obvious candidate for queening, but it takes a lot of finesse to execute this intention.

    1 P–R7   . . . .

This seems to win easily, for after 1 . . . R–N1? White has 2 B–N3ch! and 3 B–N8. But Black has tougher resistance methods.

    1 . . . .   R–N7ch

A finesse. If White's King plays up the board Black replies 2 . . . R–N1, for on 3 B–N3ch? he can capture the Bishop with a check.

    2 K–N1   R–N8ch

A puzzling situation. How does White make further progress?

    3 B–K1!   RxBch

He has no choice, for on 3 . . . R–N1; 4 B–N3ch is decisive.

    4 K–N2   R–K7ch
    5 K–N3   R–K6ch
    6 K–N4   R–K5ch
    7 K–N5 and wins

The position of Black's King is doubly important in this splendid ending—as a target for White's check, and as an obstacle to the Black Rook.

U. GANDOLFI

BLACK

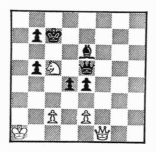

WHITE

17. White to play and win

(*See Diagram 17 on page 72*)

This study is ingenious, but more than ingenuity must have gone into it. The composer seems to have a fine sense of humor as well.

      1   Q–B4!!   ....

This sets up the Knight forking possibilities. Obviously, if 1 ... QxQ; 2 NxBch and 3 NxQ wins easily for White.

      1   ....   K–Q3
      2   NxKPch   ....

Beginning a series of checks to which Black's replies are forced.

      2   ....   K–Q4
      3   N–B6ch   K–Q3
      4   N–K8ch   K–Q4
      5   N–B7ch   K–Q3
      6   NxPch   K–Q4

So far Black has been able to hold his own, but White's next move breaks his resistance.

      7   P–B4ch!   PxP e.p.

Forced, to save his Queen. But he loses the Queen anyway.

      8   P–K4ch   QxP
      9   NxPch and wins

White forks King and Queen—the explanation of his last two mysterious-looking moves, and a diabolical windup of a clever sequence.

L. I. KUBBEL

BLACK

WHITE

18. White to play and win

(See Diagram 18 on page 73)

The key to the win will naturally be a discovered check with the Knight. But where?

1   N–B8 dis ch!   . . . .

The wealth of possibilities released by this move is nothing short of amazing. For example 1 . . . K–B1; 2 R–QB1ch, K–N1 (or 2 . . . K–Q1; 3 N–K6ch winning Black's Rook); 3 N–Q7ch, K–R2; 4 R–QR1 mate.

1   . . . .   K–K1

The only move left to Black, as 1 . . . K–B2 loses at once to 2 N–K6ch.

2   N–K6   R–N1

Again there are pretty alternatives: 2 . . . R–B2; 3 R–Q8 mate. Or 2 . . . R–R2; 3 R–Q8ch, K–B2; 4 N–N5ch and White wins.

3   N–B7ch   K–B2

4   R–KB1ch   K–N2

5   N–K6ch   K moves

6   R–KR1 mate

Thus White has echoed the mate shown in the note to his first move. How much of the beauty of chess is contained in this lovely little ending!

E. RATNER

BLACK

WHITE

19. White to play and win

(See Diagram 19 on page 74)

This ending is incredibly refined in its relentless utilization of the powers of the pieces and the exceptional subtlety of the winning procedure.

White's Bishop is attacked. If White saves the Bishop, Black moves his King, giving discovered check as a preliminary to . . . B–Q5 winning one of the Knights, after which the draw is certain.

Yet White can win.

1	B–K2!!	K–N2 dis ch

Here 1 . . . K–R4 dis ch; 2 K–N2, B–Q5 will not do, as White has 3 N–N3ch.

2	K–N2	B–Q5
3	N–N3	BxN

All this looks very unpromising for White, but it is all part of his winning plan.

4	N–R5ch!	K–R1

The only move, for on 4 . . . K–N3; 5 N–B4ch wins the Bishop; and on 4 . . . K–N1; 5 N–B6ch accomplishes the same object. Finally, if 4 . . . K–B1; 5 B–N4ch drives the King to Queen 1 or Queen Knight 1, whereupon 6 N–B6ch still wins the Bishop.

5	N–B6	. . . .

By attacking the Bishop, White gains time for tying Black's King.

5	. . . .	B–B6
6	B–R6!	. . . .

Now the stage is set for the arrival of White's King.

6	. . . .	P–N4
7	K–B3	B–Q7
8	K–N4	B–K6
9	K–B5	P–N5
10	K–K6!	P–N6
11	K–Q7	P–N7
12	K–B8	P–N8/Q
13	B–N7 mate	

Truly a gem of purest ray.

H. MATTISON, 1914

BLACK

WHITE

20. White to play and draw

White appears helpless against the coming advance of Black's King Pawn, for example 1 R–B1, P–K7 etc. Yet White has a magnificent resource which relies on no less than three stalemate possibilities!

1   R–R1   P–B8/Q!

The best chance, as 1 . . . P–K7?; 2 NxP wins for White.

2   RxQ   P–K7

Apparently decisive, for if 3 R–K1, PxN/Qch; 4 RxQ, N–K6ch followed by 5 . . . NxR and Black wins.

3   R–N1!!   PxN/R

Or 3 . . . PxN/Qch; 4 K–R3 dis ch, QxR and White is stalemated.

4   K–R5 dis ch!   N–N2ch

Or 4 . . . RxR and again White is stalemated.

5   K–R6   RxR

Still stalemate! The concentrated richness of White's resources is amazing.

L. VAN VLIET

BLACK

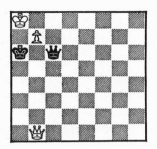

WHITE

21. White to play and win

The charm of this simple-looking study is that it artfully conceals some surprisingly beautiful winning lines. Even after we work out the solution it seems astonishing that White's fine first move can accomplish so much.

　　　1　Q–N4!!　　　....

Believe it or not, no matter how Black plays he will be compelled to give up his pin on White's Pawn, allowing it to queen. Consider these possibilities:

If Black plays 1 . . . Q–Q4 or 1 . . . Q–KB6, White wins at once with 2 Q–QR4ch, K–N6; 3 Q–N3ch!, QxQ; 4 P–N8/Qch winning Black's Queen.

Now that we have the idea, we can see that 1 . . . Q–N7 is refuted by 2 Q–R3ch, K moves; 3 Q–N2ch! etc. So Black is left with a single move:

　　　1　....　　　　Q–R8
　　　2　Q–R3ch　　　K–N3

If 2 . . . K–N4; 3 Q–N2ch and we have these two possibilities: 3 . . . K–R3; 4 Q–QR2ch followed by 5 Q–N1ch! and wins—or 3 . . . K–B5; 4 K–R7, Q–KN8ch; 5 K–R6, Q–KN3ch; 6 Q–N6 and the Pawn must queen as Black has no checks left.

3   Q–N2ch   . . . .

This does not leave Black much choice, for if 3 . . . K–B2; 4
Q–KR2ch! wins; while if 3 . . . K–B4; 4 K–R7, Q–R2; 5 Q–N6ch
followed by 6 K–R6 and again the Pawn queens as Black has no
checks.

3	. . . .	K–R3
4	Q–QR2ch	K moves
5	Q–N1ch!	QxQ
6	P–N8/Qch and wins	

White's winning method involves no less than six Queen sacrifices—
surely some kind of record for such a deceptively colorless position.

A. HERBSTMANN, 1935

BLACK

WHITE

22. *White to play and win*

White opens with a startling Queen offer. When Black declines,
White hounds the Black King until the offer must be accepted.

          1   Q–K1ch!   K–B7

For if 1 . . . KxQ; 2 NxBch and 3 NxQ wins for White. The forking motif is the key to the following play.

          2   Q–QB1ch!   K–N6
          3   Q–N2ch!   K–B5

After 3 . . . K–R5 White forces Black to take by playing 4 Q–N4ch!

          4   Q–N4ch!   K–Q4

Now the chase is continued—in reverse.

5	Q–Q6ch	K–B5
6	Q–B5ch!	K–N6
7	Q–N4ch!	K–B7

Or 7 . . . K–R7; 8 Q–N2ch! and White wins.

8	Q–N2ch!	KxQ
9	NxBch	K–B6
10	NxQ and wins	

The semicircle formed by the White Queen's checks makes an interesting pattern.

D. F. PETROV, 1960

BLACK

WHITE

23. *White to play and win*

Though White is momentarily two pieces ahead, he must apparently lose one of his Bishops, after which the ending is a draw. But in point of fact he has a refined winning method!

1	R–Q8!	P–R7

After 1 . . . RxR; 2 BxR, White has an easy win. Likewise after 1 . . . R–B5ch; 2 K–K3, R–R5; 3 B–B6, P–R7; 4 R–Q1 (or 4 B–R1), etc.

2	BxP	R–B5ch
3	K–K3	R–R5
4	B–QN3	R–N5

Still keeping both Bishops under attack. Note that 4 . . . R–R6 is answered by 5 R–Q4ch and 6 R–QN4.

     5   R–Q4ch!   RxR

White does not seem to have accomplished anything, as 6 KxR, KxB is obviously a draw.

     6   B–K7!! and wins

The Rook is trapped, for example 6 . . . R–Q2; 7 B–K6ch; or 6 . . . R–KB5; 7 B–K6ch, R–B4 (if 7 . . . K–N6; 8 B–Q6); 8 K–K4. An amazing finish.

V. and M. PLATOV, 1909

BLACK

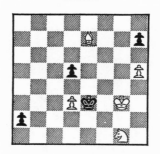

WHITE

24. White to play and win

In this ending, a marvel of intricate but clear-cut ingenuity, Black's threat to queen his Queen Rook Pawn is "only the beginning."

     1   B–B6   P–Q5

Shutting out White's Bishop, so that he apparently has nothing better than 2 N–B3, P–R8/Q; 3 BxPch, QxB; 4 NxQ, KxN; 5 K–N4—but this won't win for White!

For after 5 . . . KxP; 6 K–N5, K–K5; 7 K–R6, K–B4; 8 KxP, K–B3 White's remaining Pawn is useless for winning purposes, for example 9 P–R6, K–B3; 10 K–R8, K–B2 etc.

Instead, White must resort to an astounding move:

     2   N–K2!!   . . . .

Now if 2 . . . KxN; 3 BxP, KxP; 4 B–R1, K–K5; 5 K–N4 with an easy win for White, as he picks off the King Rook Pawn with no opposition from Black.

2 . . . .　　　　　P–R8/Q

Black expects an easy draw by 3 BxPch, QxB; 4 NxQ, KxN etc. (see above).

3 N–B1!!　　　. . . .

Fantastic—White threatens 4 B–N5 mate!

Nor does 3 . . . P–R3 help, as White replies 4 B–K5 threatening 5 B–B4 mate.

Note also that 3 . . . QxN is refuted by 4 B–N5ch winning the Queen; or 3 . . . K–Q7; 4 N–N3ch with the same result.

3 . . . .　　　　　Q–R4

This stops 4 B–N5 mate but leads to disaster by a different route:

4 BxPch!! and wins

A splendid finish. On 4 . . . K–Q7 or 4 . . . KxB White picks up the Queen with 5 N–N3ch etc. A deeply satisfying gem.

C. BEHTING, 1908

BLACK

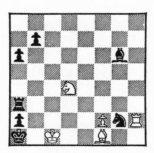

WHITE

25. White to play and win

Our point of departure here is the uneasy situation of Black's King, which is under a standing menace of N–N3 mate or N–B2 mate. What can White do to make these threats workable?

Solution: the paths of Black's Rook and Bishop coincide at Black's Queen 6 square. These pieces prevent the Knight checkmate. This, then, is White's target. But it takes some wonderfully ingenious play to bring the idea to fruition.

> 1 R–R3!!   RxR

Forced—if 1 . . . R–R5 (for example); 2 N–N3 mate.

> 2 P–B3!!   . . . .

Not 2 B–Q3? allowing Black's King to escape after 2 . . . R–R8ch.

> 2 . . . .   RxP

Again forced, to prevent N–N3 mate.

> 3 B–Q3!! and wins

For if 3 . . . BxB; 4 N–N3 mate and if 3 . . . RxB; 4 N–B2 mate. A case of "interference."

D. PETROV, 1936

BLACK

WHITE

26. *White to play and win*

A confused-looking position, with apparently no semblance of order in it. One would expect 1 NxN, KxN; 2 P–N7, R–N4; 3 RxKP with a likely draw. But of course this uninspired sequence cannot possibly be what the composer intended.

> 1 R–K7ch!   . . . .

Now we see that 1 . . . KxN is answered by 2 PxP after which the advanced White Pawn must queen. Or 1 . . . K–B1; 2 RxBP mate!

	1	K–Q3
	2 PxP	NxN

A resourceful defense. On 3 P–B8/Q Black will win the new Queen with 3 . . . N–K4ch.

But White has many surprises in store!

	3 P–B8/Nch!	K–Q4
	4 N–N6ch	K–Q3

The Black King's lack of mobility makes a sinister impression.

	5 R–Q7ch	K–K4
	6 R–Q5ch!!	. . . .

Beautiful!

	6	RxR
	7 N–B4 mate	

The Black King has been trapped in broad daylight.

H. RINCK, 1917

BLACK

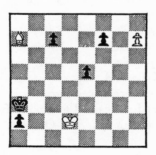

WHITE

27. *White to play and win*

If White queens, Black queens in reply and nothing has been gained for White. The winning method has to be much subtler—so much so that White's first move looks like utter madness.

	1 B–Q4!!	PxB

White's new Queen will now be in position to check at Queen Rook 8, putting Black's King in a very unfavorable position.

	2	P–R8/Q	P–R8/Q

Other moves leave White with an easy win, example 2 . . .
P–QB4; 3 Q–R1, K–N7; 4 Q–QB1ch etc.

	3	Q–R8ch	K–N7
	4	Q–N7ch	K–R7
	5	Q–R6ch	K–N8

Instead, 5 . . . K–N7; 6 Q–N5ch, K–R7; 7 Q–R4ch, K–N7;
8 QxPch wins more rapidly for White. White's objective is to bring
his Queen in closer so that Black's King is systematically deprived of
mobility.

	6	Q–Q3ch	K–R7
	7	Q–B4ch	K–R6
	8	Q–R6ch	K–N7
	9	Q–N5ch	K–R6
	10	Q–R5ch	. . . .

White is making headway against Black's best defense.

	10	. . . .	K–N7
	11	Q–N4ch	K–R2
	12	Q–R4ch	K–N7

Forced—if 12 . . . K–N8??; 13 Q–B2 mate.

	13	QxPch	K–N8
	14	Q–K4ch	K–R7
	15	Q–QR4ch	K–N7
	16	Q–QN4ch	K–R7
	17	K–B2 and wins	

With three different checkmates threatened, Black cannot escape.
Note that if White had not paused to capture Black's Queen Pawn,
Black could now escape with 17 . . . P–Q6ch!

K. A. L. KUBBEL, 1924

BLACK

WHITE

28. White to play and win

White's winning method depends on hidden threats against the Black Queen.

    1 Q–R2ch!   K–N5

Other King moves lose the Queen (for example, 1 . . . K–N4?; 2 N–B3ch). This thought applies to the next two moves as well.

    2 Q–N2ch   K–B5
    3 Q–B2ch   K–N5
    4 K–N2!   Q–Q4

Forced by White's threat of Q–N3 mate.

    5 Q–R4ch!!   . . . .

This is the sensational move that White has been leading up to.

    5 . . . .   KxQ
    6 N–B3ch   K–N5
    7 NxQch   K moves

No matter where Black plays his King, he is subject to a forking check. It is this exquisite detail that is the real point of the whole composition.

    8 N checks and wins

The Knight checks on Queen Knight 6 or Queen Bishop 7, depending on the King's previous move. White's Rook Pawn will then queen by force.

M. HAVEL, 1926

29. White to play and win

The experienced solver will at once sense the mechanism for finding the solution. Somehow White must arrange matters in such a way as to check on the long diagonal and thereby win the Black Queen. White's Queen will probably help to bring this about by checking on black squares—protected by his Bishop.

       1 Q–Q7ch   . . . .

This looks right, for 1 . . . K–K5?? allows 2 Q–B6ch winning the Queen.

The chief variation to consider is 1 . . . K–K4; 2 Q–KN7ch, K–K3; 3 Q–K7ch, K–B4; 4 Q–B6ch, K–N5; 5 Q–N5ch and Black must choose between 5 . . . K–R6; 6 Q–N3 mate and 5 . . . K–B6; 6 Q–Q5ch winning the Queen.

       1 . . . .   K–B5

If Black tries 1 . . . K–B4; 2 B–B2ch brings us to the same line of play.

       2 Q–N5ch   K–Q5

Again, if 2 . . . K–B6; 3 B–K1ch! leads to the same line of play.

       3 B–B2ch   K–B6

Not 3 . . . K–K5??; 4 Q–B6ch etc.

       4 B–K1ch!   K–Q5

Or 4 . . . QxB??; 5 Q–N4ch winning the Queen. If 4 . . . K–N7;

5 Q–K2ch with this likely finish: 5 . . . K–B8; 6 Q–Q2ch, K–N8; 7 Q–Q1ch, K–R7 forced; 8 Q–B2ch and mate next move.

          5   Q–N2ch   K–B4

If 5 . . . K–Q4?? or . . . K–K5??; 6 Q–QN7ch wins Black's Queen. On 5 . . . K–B5; 6 Q–N4ch leads into the main line. If 5 . . . K–K6; 6 Q–B1ch! wins, as 6 . . . K–K5?? or 5 . . . K–Q5?? loses the Queen, while 6 . . . K–Q6; 7 Q–B3ch leads into the main line.

          6   Q–N6ch   K–B5

Forced.

          7   Q–N4ch   K–Q6

Again forced.

          8   Q–B3ch   K–K7

Still forced.

          9   Q–Q2ch and wins

White must lose his Queen or get mated. We have here the same position as in the first note, except that the position is at right angles to the one given there. Astonishingly varied play for such a bare setting.

G. KASPARYAN, 1935

BLACK

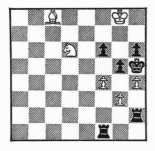

WHITE

30. *White to play and win*

This position has been cunningly constructed to afford a wealth of checkmating possibilities.

1   N–K8   . . . .

White threatens 2 N–N7ch, K–N3; 3 B–B5 mate.

1   . . . .   K–N3

Here 1 . . . P–B4 is no defense, as White simply plays 2 BxP followed by 3 N–N7 mate.

2   P–R5ch!   . . . .

This leaves Black no choice, for if 2 . . . KxP; 3 N–N7ch and 4 B–B5 mate.

2   . . . .   RxP

3   P–B5ch!   RxP

4   P–N4   R–B4

White was threatening 5 BxR mate or 5 PxR/B5 mate.

5   B–B5ch!!   RxB

6   N–N7!! and wins

No matter which Rook moves, the reply is 7 PxR mate. A fiendishly clever study.

Chess Problems

As in the case of end game studies, we have here a little world, self-contained and independent. Few chess players are familiar with it and fewer still are attuned to its beauties. But it is a world that is singularly rewarding.

It would make me happy to know that my arguments in favor of problems in an earlier book, *How to Get More Out of Chess,* have brought some converts into the fold. There I wrote:

"Many problem ideas and mating techniques have an inherent beauty that is irresistible to any lover of artistry in chess. Once you're bitten by the problem 'bug,' it never lets go of you.

"But there is another element in problems that appeals to us. When we play a game with an opponent, we want to win. We also want to play beautiful, interesting chess. Sometimes these aims get into each other's way. We may win, but in the process we may produce a game on which our verdict is: 'Putrid!'

"On the other hand, we may play a beautiful game, and botch it at the very end. What chess player is not grieved by such an unfortunate outcome?

"In the realm of problems this competitive angle is ruled out, and that is the way some of us prefer it. We are perfectly free to enjoy the beauty of chess without indulging in pernicious rivalry and petty spite."

What can be added to this? Study these problems, enjoy them, admire them. And perhaps you will become a convert too.

(See Diagram 1 on page 90)

An uproarious situation—but not for Black, who, despite his enormous advantage in material, is helpless as a babe:

1	P–Q8/N!	any
2	N–B7 mate	

One for the books.

C. S. KIPPING

BLACK

WHITE

1. White to play and mate in 2 moves

I. DEMESHONOK, 1958

BLACK

WHITE

2. White to play and mate in 2 moves

(See Diagram 2 on page 90)

The key is a waiting move, which means that White must create the maximum of power for his forces. The move that answers the purpose is *1 Q–Q5!* leaving Black helpless.

If Black plays 1 . . . B–N2 (blocking his King's retreat to King Knight 2), White replies 2 B–N5 mate.

If Black plays 1 . . . P–K3 (depriving his King of a flight square), White replies 2 Q–KN5 mate.

If Black plays 1 . . . P–K4 (depriving his King of a different flight square), White replies 2 Q–B7 mate.

The fewness of the forces involved leads to attractively clean-cut play.

A. C. WHITE, 1918

BLACK

WHITE

3. White to play and mate in 2 moves

This is a fine example of a waiting key. White's first move threatens nothing, but every Black reply allows a new mate to arise.

      1 R–QN4!   . . . .

If Black moves his Bishop (opening a line for White's Queen), White replies 2 Q–R7 mate.

If Black plays 1 . . . Q–Q5 (blocking his Bishop's diagonal), White replies 2 R–N3 mate.

If Black plays 1 . . . Q–Q4 (releasing the pin on White's Bishop), White replies 2 B–N5 mate.

If Black plays 1 . . . P–K4 (opening a line for White's Queen), White replies 2 Q–R3 mate.

If Black plays 1 . . . QxQ (unpinning White's Bishop), White replies 2 B–K4 mate.

It is always a pleasure to see such clean-cut variations on an uncluttered board.

S. LOYD, 1867

BLACK

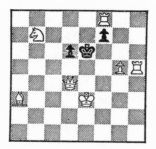

WHITE

4. White to play and mate in 2 moves

Solvers who remember the convention that the key move should not be a check have gone quietly mad over this problem. The key prepared by the fun-loving composer is *1 Q–KN4ch!*

If Black plays 1 . . . K–K2, White replies 2 BxP mate.

If Black plays 1 . . . K–K4 or 1 . . . K–Q4, White replies 2 Q–K4 mate.

If Black plays 1 . . . P–B4, White replies 2 PxP *e.p.* mate! Note that the *en passant* capture opens up the fifth rank for White's Rook at King Rook 5.

After all these years this old problem still retains its sting.

A. C. WHITE, 1920

BLACK

WHITE

5. White to play and mate in 2 moves

Though the key is a waiting move, it is anything but inactive. In fact, it has substantial claims to being the most astonishing key in the whole realm of problems: *1 Q–R1!!*

If Black plays 1 . . . QxQch or 1 . . . B–N7ch, White replies 2 P–B3 mate.

If Black plays 1 . . . Q–N7ch, White replies 2 B–B3 mate.

If Black plays 1 . . . BxB, White replies 2 QxQ mate.

(*See Diagram 6 on page 95*)

This is the kind of problem which despite its tantalizing appearance of simplicity nevertheless gives the solver trouble—and then fills him with chagrin because it's essentially very easy.

        1   Q–QN2!   . . . .

A waiting move that puts the Queen on the right diagonal.

        1   . . . .   K–R8

Now White's King approaches, but of course not by 2 K–B1?? which is stalemate.

        2   K–B2!   K–R7
        3   Q–R8 mate

Very easy, after all.

B. LARSEN

BLACK

WHITE

6. White to play and mate in 3 moves

V. HEBEL, 1959

BLACK

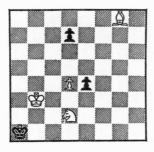

WHITE

7. White to play and mate in 3 moves

The stalemate position of Black's King suggests that White must provide for the three possible Pawn moves at Black's disposal. The solution, as will be seen, hinges on the possibility of N–N3ch without allowing the Black monarch to escape. To make the Knight check possible (*see Diagram 7*), we need *1 K–R3!* with these variations:

I

1	. . . .	P–Q3
2	B–R2	any
3	N–N3 mate	

II

1	. . . .	P–Q4
2	B–R7	P–K6
3	N–N3 mate	

III

1	. . . .	P–K6
2	N–N3ch	K–N8
3	B–R7 mate	

E. GROSS, 1960

BLACK

WHITE

8. *White to play and mate in 3 moves*

(See Diagram 8 on page 96)

This easy but delightful problem was inspired by the procedure from Diagram 37 (page 149).

1	Q–N8!	. . . .
	Very surprising—he allows a discovered check.

1	. . . .	PxB dis ch
2	R–B6ch!	KxR
3	Q–Q6 mate	

J. FULPIUS, 1959

BLACK

WHITE

9. White to play and mate in 3 moves

This looks absurdly easy, but there is more than meets the eye. The first move has to be a Bishop move:

1	B–R4	. . . .

Threatens 2 Q–Q1 mate.

1	. . . .	R–KN6!

Black poses a dilemma. 2 KxR allows the Black King to escape, while 2 BxR? stalemates Black.

2	KxR!	K–K8

This flight is short-lived, as White has a deadly discovered check.

3	K–N7 mate

The masking and unmasking of the Bishop's diagonal provide an elegant touch.

T. R. DAWSON

BLACK

WHITE

10. White to play and mate in 3 moves

The composer's clever handling of the scattered White pieces has been called a *tour de force*. Two factors stand out: Black's King is limited to the King Rook file; and White's Knight must play an active role. The *key* is 1 N–B5. There are then two main possibilities:

If Black plays 1 . . . K–R5, White replies 2 N–K4, K–R6; 3 Q–N3 mate. Or 2 . . . K–R4; 3 Q–N5 mate.

If Black plays 1 . . . K–R3, White replies 2 N–K6, K–R2, Q–N7 mate. Or 2 . . . K–R4; 3 Q–N5 mate. The echo motif is a nice touch.

A. C. WHITE, 1913

BLACK

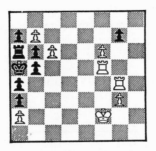

WHITE

11. White to play and mate in 3 moves

A delightful study in underpromotion. The key move is 1 P–N8/B!
and there are three possibilities:

I

1 . . . .   PxP
2 B–B4   . . . .

An important move, to give Black's King a flight square. (If White
had promoted to a Queen, Black would now be stalemated.)

2 . . . .   K–N5
3 B–Q2 mate

II

1 . . . .   P–N3
2 B–Q6   . . . .

This is possible here because Black has a spare move and thus stalemate is averted.

2 . . . .   PxR
3 B–N4 mate

III

1 . . . .   P–N4

As in Variation I, Black is depriving himself of moves; therefore White again blocks the action of one of his Rooks.

2 B–K5   P–N5
3 B–B7 mate

A beautiful point here is that Black is unable to reply 3 . . . P–N4. This unobtrusive problem conceals a good deal of artistry.

S. LOYD, 1867

BLACK

WHITE

12. *White to play and mate in 3 moves*

As we have seen, Loyd was no respecter of the canons that govern problem composing. The *key* here is a capture: 1 PxB. But the promotion is a ticklish problem. If White promotes to a Queen, Rook or Bishop, Black replies 1 . . . R–R3 and it is impossible for White to checkmate in the prescribed number of moves. The right way is:

1 PxB/N!!   . . . .

If Black's Rook moves off the rank, White replies 2 QxN mate. If Black's Rook moves indiscriminately on the rank, White replies 2 Q–R1ch followed by mate next move. There remains only:

1 . . . .   R–R3
2 N–N6!   . . . .

White threatens 3 QxN mate. If Black plays 2 . . . RxN there follows 3 Q–R1 mate.

White's second move is a fine example of "interference." Black's Rook is rendered useless.

S. LOYD, 1876

BLACK

WHITE

13. White to play and mate in 3 moves

Here too Loyd was not afraid to violate the canon that the first move must not be a capture. The solution involves 1 PxB. But how is White to promote? If he chooses a Queen or Bishop, Black is stalemated. But 1 PxB/R, KxN will not do either, for then Black is set to play 2 . . . BxP, dispelling all hopes of a checkmate. No, the promotion must be more subtle:

    1   PxB/N!!   . . . .

The beauty of this move is that it works although it looks utterly idiotic.

    1   . . . .   KxN
    2   N–N6!!   . . . .

White threatens to promote the other Pawn and at the same time prevents 2 . . . BxP. Now we see why the Knight promotion was needed. No matter how Black plays, White's next move is: 3 P–R8/Q mate or 3 P–R8/B mate.

W. VON HOLTZHAUSEN, 1923

BLACK

WHITE

14. White to play and mate in 3 moves

White's task is harder than it seems. After the obvious 1 P–B8/Qch, B–N1 the stalemate danger makes it impossible to force mate in the prescribed number of moves. The right way is:

    1 R–B4!!   . . . .

Momentarily shutting off the Bishop and thus threatening to promote the advanced Pawn with checkmate. If now 1 . . . K–N1; 2 P–B8/Qch, K–B2; 3 R–B7 mate.

    1 . . . .   BxR
    2 P–B8/Qch   B–N1
    3 Q–B3 mate

Very pretty. The purpose of White's first move, then, is get rid of the Rook so as to clear the file for the later Queen check.

(*See Diagram 15 on page 103*)

The fine unpinning key leads to some delightful surprises:

    1 R–R3!!!   NxR

Or 1 . . . B–B7; 2 Q–N4!!, PxQ; 3 P–R5 mate! This explains White's fantastic Rook move.

    2 QxRPch!   KxQ
    3 B–B7 mate

Truly a triumph of imagination.

D. PRZEPIORKA, 1911

BLACK

WHITE

15. White to play and mate in 3 moves

E. RICHTER, 1960

BLACK

WHITE

16. White to play and mate in 4 moves

In order to solve this problem (*Diagram 16 on page 103*) you must lift the stalemate threat. The solution:

1	B–B4	PxB
2	P–N3	PxP
3	R–KR2ch	PxR
4	N–B2 mate	

White's playful preparations lead to a surprise mate.

F. PALATZ, 1940

BLACK

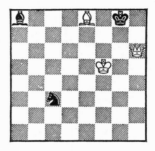

WHITE

17. White to play and mate in 4 moves

Before White's difficulties are explained, this problem looks easy. After they are explained, it looks hard. Yet it yields readily enough to logical analysis.

With 1 K–K6 or 1 K–B6 or 1 K–N6, White threatens 2 B–B7 mate; and with 1 K–B6 or 1 K–N6, White also threatens 2 Q–N7 mate. Which is the right King move?

It is clear that 1 K–N6, B–K5ch; 2 K–B6, N–Q4ch; 3 K–K6, N–B2ch does not do the trick. Likewise after 1 K–B6, N–Q4ch!; 2 K–N6, N–K2ch or 2 K–K6, N–B2ch White fails to make headway.

The right course is:

1	K–K6!	B–Q4ch

He must stop 2 B–B7 mate.

2	K–B6	N–K5ch

Again the only move to stop mate.

    3   K–N6   . . . .

Now Black has run out of checks and it is mate next move.

A. KRAEMER, 1926

BLACK

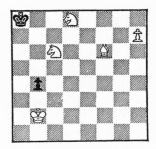

WHITE

18. White to play and mate in 4 moves

The situation of Black's King tells us at a glance that White must avoid stalemate possibilities. By retreating his own King, White gives the Black Pawn an extra move and also prepares a fine mating sequence:

    1   K–N1   P–N6

    2   B–R1!   P–N7

    3   P–R8/Q   PxB/Qch

    4   QxQ mate

Of course it does not matter how Black promotes at move 3. The main thing is that the White Queen is able to recapture and give checkmate.

(*See Diagram 19 on page 106*)

This problem turns out to be harder than it looks. If 1 NxR or 1 RxR, Black is stalemated.

There is a plausible try in 1 R–R7ch, RxR; 2 N–B3 (threatening 3 N–N5 mate), R–R4; and White has no mating moves. For example, if 3 K–R2, P–R6! (any Rook move allows White to force mate on the fourth move).

D. PRZEPIORKA, 1911

BLACK

WHITE

19. White to play and mate in 4 moves

Here is the solution:

        1 R–N5   . . . .

Threatens 2 R–R5 mate.

        1 . . . .   R–B4

If 1 . . . R–R2; 2 R–R5ch! forces mate as in the main line.

        2 R–R5ch!   . . . .

Not 2 RxR? and Black is stalemated.

        2 . . . .   RxR

        3 N–B3   . . . .

Now White can force mate on the next move. If Black's Rook makes a vertical move, White continues 4 N–N5 mate. If the Black Rook makes a horizontal move, White continues 4 R–R4 mate.

W. PAULY

BLACK

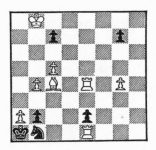

WHITE

20. White to play and mate in 4 moves

The many beauties of this masterpiece become gradually recognizable after you have studied it for a while. Black's King is in a stalemate position and he is left with only three Pawn moves. The key move is *1 R–K7!* with these possibilities:

I

1	. . . .	P–N3
2	R–R7!	any
3	R/R7–R1	any
4	RxN mate	

The other lines are more difficult:

II

1	. . . .	P–N4
2	B–N8!	. . . .

It would not do to play 2 R–R7, P–B3; 3 R/R7–R1 and Black is stalemated.

2	. . . .	P–B3
3	R–KB7!	. . . .

This relieves the stalemate.

    3   . . . .   KxP
    4   R–QR7 mate

III

    1   . . . .   P–B3
    2   R–QR7   P–N4

Again setting up a stalemate position. If instead 2 . . . P–N3; 3 B–Q3, P–N4; 4 RxN mate.

    3   B–R6!   KxP
    4   B–B4 mate

Truly a gem.

D. PRZEPIORKA, 1913

BLACK

WHITE

21. White to play and mate in 5 moves

A very attractive problem. It is obvious that White must set up the mechanism B–R6 followed by B–N7 mate. However, the immediate 1 B–R6 is parried by 1 . . . Q–N7. Hence the decisive maneuver requires preparation.

White might therefore try 1 Q–K4ch!?, NxQ; 2 B–R6. But even though Black's Queen is blocked off, he can still meet the threat easily with 2 . . . N–B4 or 2 . . . N–Q3ch. So something more subtle is called for.

Perhaps 1 Q–N6 (threatening 2 Q–QB6 mate) is the move, as it provokes 1 . . . B–Q3, depriving Black of the possibility of a later . . . N–Q3ch. Then White plays 2 Q–B2, hoping for 2 . . . P–B4?; 3 Q–K4ch!, NxQ; 4 B–R6 forcing mate next move, as Black's defensive moves with the Knight are ruled out.

All very ingenious, but after 1 Q–N6, B–Q3; 2 Q–B2, Black plays 2 . . . B–B4! so that after 3 Q–K4ch?, NxQ; 4 B–R6, Black escapes with 4 . . . N–Q3ch.

We can now appreciate the subtlety of the solution:

    1   Q–B2!   P–B4

Forced, as . . . B–B4 is not available. But now Black's Knight is cut off from one of the vital defensive squares.

    2   Q–N6!   B–Q3

Again forced, but now Black's Knight has been deprived of the other vital defensive square.

    3   Q–K4ch!   NxQ

Now Black's Queen is blocked off the diagonal.

    4   B–R6   any
    5   B–N7 mate

A gem of flawless strategy.

S. RUBIN, 1960

BLACK

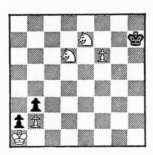

WHITE

22. *White to play and mate in 6 moves*

A witty example of underpromotion leading to an unconventional mate:

1	N/Q6–B5	K–R1
2	P–B7	K–R2

Now promoting to a Queen or Rook leads to immediate stalemate, while promoting to a Bishop does not checkmate in the prescribed number of moves.

3	P–B8/Nch!	K–R1
4	N–Q7	K–R2
5	N–B6ch	K–R1
6	N–N6 mate	

An amusing tableau.

M. NIEMEIJER, 1937

BLACK

WHITE

23. White to play and mate in 6 moves

This problem is as logical as it is engaging. White obviously carries out his idea by B–R6 and B–N7 mate. However, the immediate 1 B–R6 fails because of 1 . . . RxKNP. The preparatory 1 B–N5 (intending 2 B–B6 mate) fails by reason of 2 . . . R–N3! (but not 2 . . . R–KB8??; 3 B–R6 forcing mate).

So we go back a step further with the idea of enticing Black's Pawn forward by playing 1 B–B4 (hoping for 1 . . . P–Q3; 2 B–N5,

R–KB8; 3 B–R6 etc.). However, Black slyly defends with 1 . . . R–N4!

So perhaps the right idea is to play 1 B–K3, threatening 2 B–Q4 and thereby provoking 1 . . . P–QB4?, whereupon 2 B–B4 works as Black can no longer reply . . . R–N4. But Black meets 1 B–K3 with 1 . . . RxQNP still holding the position.

Thus we finally come to the right way:

> 1 B–Q2!   . . . .

Threatens 2 B–B3ch, P–KB3; 3 BxP mate (or 3 N–N6 mate).

> 1 . . . .   PxP
> 2 B–K3!   . . . .

Now that 2 . . . RxP has been ruled out, Black must advance his Queen Bishop Pawn.

> 2 . . . .   P–QB4
> 3 B–B4   . . . .

Threatens 4 B–K5ch etc. and Black is unable to parry with 3 . . . R–N4.

> 3 . . . .   P–Q3
> 4 B–N5   . . . .

Threatens 5 B–B6ch etc. and Black is unable to defend with 4 . . . R–N3.

> 4 . . . .   R–KB8
> 5 B–R6   any
> 6 B–N7 mate

The stairway motif is attractive.

D. PRZEPIORKA, 1915

BLACK

WHITE

24. White to play and mate in 7 moves

This position will be recognized as having a certain kinship with Diagram 23 (page 110). White's general idea is to play P–N6 followed by P–N7 mate, but this is easier said than done. For example, 1 P–N6?? is answered by 1 . . . Q–B8ch forcing mate! So White's basic idea must be to block this crucial diagonal.

Hence 1 Q–K2 suggests itself. But after 1 . . . PxQ; 2 P–N6, Black has a satisfactory defense in 2 . . . R–QN6! So we conclude that the Rook must be enticed away from this rank.

This leads us to consider 1 Q–B3, P–QB4; 2 Q–Q2, R–R4; 3 Q–K2, PxQ; 4 P–N6, but now Black's Queen saves the day after 4 . . . P–Q5. So we must find some way to prevent Black's Queen Pawn from advancing. Here is the solution:

    1   Q–B3   . . . .
Threatens 2 QxQBP mate.

    1   . . . .   P–QB4
If 1 . . . N–B5; 2 P–N6 wins at once, as . . . Q–B8ch is ruled out.

    2   Q–K3!   . . . .
This is the move that does the trick. By threatening 3 Q–K8 mate, White induces the blocking of a vital defensive line.

$$
\begin{array}{lll}
2 & \dots & B\text{--}K4 \\
3 & Q\text{--}Q2 & B\text{--}Q5
\end{array}
$$

If 3 . . . P–Q5; 4 Q–R2! (threatens Q–N8 mate), P–B5; 5 P–N6 etc. (Again . . . Q–B8ch has been ruled out.)

$$
\begin{array}{lll}
4 & Q\text{--}R2 & R\text{--}R4
\end{array}
$$

Again if 4 . . . N–B5; 5 P–N6 is decisive, as . . . Q–B8ch is not available.

$$
\begin{array}{lll}
5 & Q\text{--}K2! & PxQ \\
6 & P\text{--}N6 & any
\end{array}
$$

Black cannot play . . . Q–B8ch, nor can he advance his Queen Pawn to stop P–N7 mate.

$$
\begin{array}{lll}
7 & P\text{--}N7 & mate
\end{array}
$$

A triumph of logic.

K. BAYER, 1856

BLACK

WHITE

25. White to play and mate in 9 moves

An old-time classic in which White sacrifices everything but a lone Pawn!

$$
\begin{array}{lll}
1 & R\text{--}N7! & QxR \\
2 & BxPch! & KxB \\
3 & Q\text{--}KN8ch! & KxN
\end{array}
$$

4	Q–N4ch	K–K4
5	Q–R5ch	R–B4
6	P–B4ch!	BxP
7	QxNch!	BxQ
8	R–K4ch!	PxR
9	P–Q4 mate	

F. HARIUC, 1960

BLACK

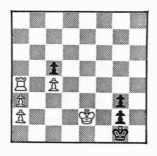

WHITE

26. White to play and mate in 16 moves

White's task is much less terrifying than it sounds, and this is really a jest rather than a problem. White must gain time to queen his Rook Pawn without allowing Black to queen his Knight Pawn.

1 R–R7!   . . . .

The only move that will do the trick.

1 . . . .   K–R7

2 R–R7ch   K–N8

Now White must relieve the stalemate position. Then he will be ready for the "windmill" process that will ensure the queening of his Pawn.

3 K–Q2!   K–B7

Threatening to queen.

4	R–KB7ch	K–N8

End of threat.

5	P–R4	K–R7
6	R–KR7ch	K–N8
7	P–R5	K–B7
8	R–KB7ch	K–N8
9	P–R6	K–R7
10	R–KR7ch	K–N8
11	P–R7	K–B7
12	R–KB7ch	K–N8
13	P–R8/Q	K–R7

If White had played 1 R–R8, he would now be unable to play 14 Q–R8ch.

14	Q–R8ch	K–N8

And here you must note that if White had played 1 R–R6 he would now be unable to play 15 Q–QR1ch, as his Rook would now be on King Bishop 6.

15	Q–QR1ch	K–R7
16	R–KR7 mate	

The "windmill" was in fine working order.

"I had a foolproof plan to win, but you didn't play your pieces
the way I expected you to."

Beautiful Combinations

Beautiful combination play is the soul of chess. The finest positional chess, if not enlivened by some tactical spark, is likely to leave us cold and make us feel that we have been cheated. Such is the popular impression, and in this case *vox populi* proclaims its views with some justice.

Long ago Réti explained why this is so:

"A combination composed of a sacrifice," he wrote, "has a more immediate effect upon the person playing over the game in which it occurs than another combination, because the apparent senselessness of the sacrifice is a convincing proof of the design of the player offering it. Hence it comes that the risk of material, and the victory of the weaker material over the stronger material, gives the impression of a symbol of the mastery of mind over matter.

"Now we see wherein lies the pleasure to be derived from a chess combination. It lies in the feeling that a human mind is behind the game dominating the inanimate pieces with which the game is carried on, and giving them the breath of life. We may regard it as an intellectual delight, equal to that afforded us by the knowledge that behind so many apparently disconnected and seemingly chance happenings in the physical world lies the one great ruling spirit—the law of Nature."

Emanuel Lasker put it in more imaginative terms:

"The most usual of all [combinative] motifs is the weakness of a piece of little or no mobility. . . . To name this motif, let us emphasize the two ideas underlying it: the idea of superior force at a given point, and that of immobility. What is immobile must suffer violence. The light-winged bird will easily escape the huge dragon, but the firmly rooted big tree must remain where it is and may have to give up its leaves, fruit, perhaps its life."

Mobility! There's the magic word. Look for this theme in these delightful combinations.

GRUENFELD–TARRASCH
Baden-Baden, 1925

BLACK

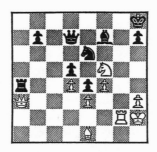

WHITE

1. White to play

White has such a formidable attacking position that he does not even bother to remove his menaced Queen from the threatened capture.

1   B–R4!!   . . . .

Threatens immediate destruction with 2 B–B6ch etc. On 1 . . . RxQ, White continues 2 B–B6ch, N–N2; 3 BxNch, K–N1; 4 N–R6 mate.

Note that 1 . . . B–N3 offers no hope of balm in Gilead, for then follows: 2 B–B6ch, K–N1; 3 N–R6 mate. So Black tries another way, which meets with a hair-raising refutation.

1   . . . .   P–R3
2   Q–B8ch!!   . . . .

This striking move knocks the props from under Black's desperate attempt to keep the Knight file closed.

2   . . . .   NxQ
3   B–B6ch   K–R2
4   R–N7ch   K–R1
5   RxB dis ch   K–N1
6   N–R6 mate

SOLDATENKOV–WOLF
Berlin, 1925

BLACK

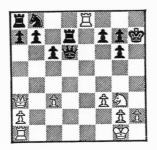

WHITE

2. *White to play*

Our first thought is that White will avoid the exchange of Queens because he is a Pawn down. Paradoxically, White gives up his Queen altogether!

	1	N–K4!!	QxQ

Retreat is of no avail: for example 1 . . . Q–B2; 2 Q–B8 and Black must resign.

	2	N–N5ch	K–R3
	3	P–R4	R–Q1

Black is coming to the bitter realization that the White Queen was not a present. He has to work hard to meet the threat of R–R8 mate.

	4	RxR	N–Q2
	5	RxR	N–B1
	6	R–Q1	QxP

With White's R/Q1–Q8 prepared, Black is definitely on the skids.

	7	RxN!	Q–B4ch

Pretty crafty, isn't he?

	8	K–R2	QxR
	9	R–Q8!	. . . .

Decisive, as Black must capture, walking into a pretty Knight fork.

9 . . . .   QxR
10 NxPch and wins
The win of the Queen leaves White a piece ahead.

WOLF–SPIELMANN
Maehrisch-Ostrau, 1923

BLACK

WHITE

3. White to play

White's advantage of the Exchange gives him an easy victory in any case, but he prefers to win by an inspired stratagem.

1 P–KR3!   . . . .

The charm of this move lies in its seeming pointlessness.

1 . . . .   QxRP

Forced.

2 QxP!!   Resigns

Now the apparent uselessness of White's previous move is explained. After 2 . . . RxQ (Black has no choice—two of his pieces are attacked); 3 R–B8ch!, BxR; 4 R–K8ch, it is mate next move.

(*See Diagram 4 on page 121*)

Black can protect his attacked Bishop in a number of ways, but his mind is traveling in totally different channels. Counterattack is the best defense, they say, and here is a fine case in point.

GOGLIDZE–BOTVINNIK
Moscow, 1935

BLACK

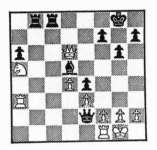

WHITE

4. White to play

| 1 | . . . . | QxRch! |
| 2 | KxQ | R–N8ch |

Or . . . R–B8ch followed by . . . R–N7 mate.

| 3 | K–K2 | R–B7 mate |

Only now do we realize how badly dispersed the White pieces are.
(*See Diagram 5 on page 122*)

To the uninitiated it might seem that White has a devastating attack. The fact is, however, that Black has a forced win. It begins with a "little" Pawn move:

| 1 | . . . . | P–B7ch! |

Forking King and Rook and, better yet threatening . . . QxP mate. White's reply is forced.

| 2 | QxP | RxRch |

The immediate . . . B–N3 also wins.

| 3 | RxR | B–N3 |
| | Resigns | |

For after 4 B–Q4, BxB, White's Queen is still rooted to the spot because of Black's . . . QxP mate threat. The "little" Pawn check was White's undoing.

ROMIH–SZABADOS
Italian Championship, 1952

BLACK

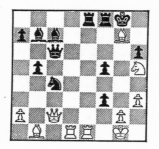

WHITE

5. Black to play

BALDANELLO–PRIMAVERA
Italian Championship, 1952

BLACK

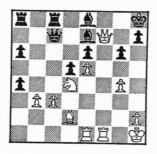

WHITE

6. White to play

(*See Diagram 6 on page 122*)

"The better," said Plato, "is the enemy of the good." Like so many wise old saws, this impressive-sounding maxim has many loopholes. This is particularly true of chess, where the good is often the enemy of the better. For example: White has a good move in 1 QxKP, which is certainly adequate for winning purposes. But he has another move which is incomparably better:

1	Q–B8ch!!	Resigns

For after 1 . . . BxQ; 2 RxBch, K–N2 there follows 3 NxP mate. Q.E.D.

BOGOLYUBOV–RUBINSTEIN
Bad Kissingen, 1928

BLACK

WHITE

7. *White to play*

With so many White pieces admirably poised for attack, and with Black's King-side denuded of defensive forces, White has all the necessary makings of a withering attack.

1	BxPch!	KxB
2	Q–R5ch	K–N1

Perhaps Black expected 3 NxP here. It is good enough to win, but White has an alternative that is more conclusive.

3	N–N6!	Resigns

White's last move is murderous. He threatens 4 Q–R8 mate. And if Black tries 3 . . . PxN he runs into 4 RxR mate.

SAMUELSSON–HILDEBRAND
Halmstad, 1951

BLACK

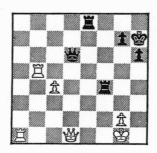

WHITE

8. *Black to play*

It takes a real flair to pull off a coup in as colorless-looking a position as this one. One expects 1 . . . QxQch; 2 RxQ, RxP; and although Black is a Pawn ahead, White's drawing chances are quite considerable. But Black has much better:

1	. . . .	R–K8ch!!
2	QxR	Q–Q5ch
3	K–R1	. . . .

The alternative 3 K–R2, R–R5ch leads into the main line, for if 4 K–N3, Q–B5 mate.

3	. . . .	R–R5ch
4	QxR	QxQch
5	K–N1	. . . .

Now comes the real point of Black's combination:

| 5 | . . . . | Q–Q5ch |
| | Resigns | |

For he must lose a Rook. All very nicely calculated by Black.

ROSSETTO–FLORES
Mar del Plata, 1951

BLACK

WHITE

9. Black to play

A difficult position to appraise. It is obvious that on 1 . . . BxN
White will lose a piece if he replies 2 PxB? Instead he plays 2 B–B4,
continuing with 3 PxB after the retreat of Black's Queen. In that
event White's strong passed Pawn should give him a distinctly preferable game—not to mention the fact that the situation of Black's Knight
is on the precarious side.

All very logical, yet Black plays:

    1 . . . .   BxN!

Forcing White's hand.

    2 B–B4   QxP!!

    Resigns

For after 3 BxQ, BxBch White has the sorry choice between 4
K–N1, N–K7 mate and 4 R–B3, BxRch and Black ends up with an
enormous plus in material. Who said chess is a logical game?!

(See Diagram 10 on page 126)

Effective combinations often depend on a move that is hard to
find yet seems absurdly simple once it has been found. Here is a perfect
case in point: the immediate 1 Q–R3ch is not directly decisive be-

GUIMARD–WEXLER
Mar del Plata, 1951

BLACK

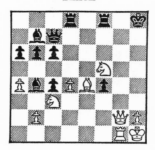

WHITE

10. White to play

cause of 1 . . . Q–R2. Yet there *is* a way for White to make dynamic use of all the open lines:

1 N–K7!!   Resigns

Black is helpless against the double threat of 2 Q–N7 mate or 2 Q–R3 mate. Thus, if 1 . . . QxN; 2 Q–R3ch and mate next move. An artful—and artistic—conclusion.

(*See Diagram 11 on page 127*)

On the face of it, a disastrous situation for White, who is subjected to a seemingly crushing double attack. Actually, he has a clever win.

1 RxN!   . . . .

Proving that Black's double attack on the White Queen and Rook was really a sham.

1 . . . .   PxQ

He can stop mate only at the cost of remaining a piece down.

2 RxPch   K–R1
3 RxBP dis ch   K–N1
4 R–KN7ch   K–R1
5 R–N3 dis ch   Resigns

It is mate in two more moves. A revelation of the power of the long diagonal.

RESHEVSKY–SHAINSWIT
New York, 1951

BLACK

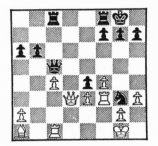

WHITE

11. White to play

MADERNA–ROSSETTO
Mar del Plata, 1951

BLACK

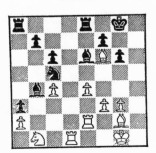

WHITE

12. White to play

(See Diagram 12 on page 127)

With the Queens gone, a long-drawn-out ending is apparently in sight. Instead, a nonsensical-looking move forces a remarkably quick decision for White.

      1 B–B1!!   Resigns

For Black sees that he is in a mating net. If 1 . . . BxP; 2 R–R2 forces mate (this is the threat in any event). Nor does 1 . . . N–Q2 bring any relief, as White has the brutal rejoinder 2 RxN, BxR; 3 R–R2 etc.

Incidentally, 1 B–R1!! would also have been decisive.

Such virulent mating possibilities with the Queens removed are rather unusual.

ARONSSON–WADLING
Swedish tournament, 1951

BLACK

WHITE

13. White to play

Once more the classic refrain: Black pays a heavy price for having put his Queen out of play; and of course the undeveloped state of Black's Queen-side pieces only makes matters worse for him.

      1 BxPch!   . . . .

This sudden raiding attack is conclusive. Black's reply is forced, for if 1 . . . K–R1; 2 N–B7 mate.

      1 . . . .   NxB

      2 Q–N6!   . . . .

Again leaving Black no choice, for if 2 . . . R–Q1 (or . . . Q–Q1); 3 Q–B7ch, K–R1; 4 N–N6 mate—or 2 . . . R–B1; 3 N–R5 again forcing mate.

2	. . . .	PxN
3	QxRch	B–B1
4	BPxP	N–N3
5	N–R5	. . . .

With a very neat turn in mind.

5	. . . .	B–Q2
6	RxBch!	NxR
7	Q–K7	Resigns

Mate is forced after all.

SZABO–SNAEVARR
Munich, 1936

BLACK

WHITE

14. White to play

Black has fatally weakened his King's position with indiscriminate Pawn moves. Despite the seeming solidity of his position he is helpless against White's cleverly executed attack:

    1 BxN!   R–Q8ch

Black interpolates this check in order to lure White's Queen Bishop off the long diagonal, but even with this would-be resource he cannot break the force of White's attack.

2	R–K1	RxRch
3	BxR	KxB
4	QxPch!!	. . . .

A rude shock for Black. If 4 . . . PxQ; 5 NxBPch and mate next move.

4	. . . .	K–N1
5	NxPch	K–B2
6	Q–N6ch	Resigns

Black must suffer murderous material loss.

AMATEUR-BENDINGER
Munich, 1939

BLACK

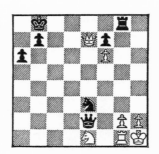

WHITE

15. Black to play

Black's startling Queen sacrifice is merely the prelude to a second sacrifice:

1	. . . .	N–B4!!

To this White has no satisfactory reply.

2	QxQ	N–N6ch!
3	PxN	R–R1ch
4	Q–R5	RxQ mate

The White King's snug retreat turned out to be too crowded.

WADE–LOKVENC
England–Austria, 1959

BLACK

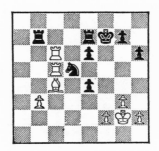

WHITE

16. White to play

White's simple winning line is very impressive after all.

    1   RxN!   . . . .

There is more in this move than meets the eye.

    1   . . . .   PxR

    2   BxPch   Resigns

No matter how Black plays he comes out a Rook down! Proof: if
2 . . . K–K1 (or 2 . . . K–B1; 3 R–B8ch with the same result); 3
R–B8ch, K–Q2; 4 BxR. This shows the hand of the master!

(*See Diagram 17 on page 132*)

White's relentless harping on the last rank reduces Black to complete
helplessness.

    1   Q–Q2!   . . . .

Naturally Black cannot reply 1 . . . QxQ because of 2 R–K8 mate.

Nor will 1 . . . Q–R1 do because of 2 Q–R5!, Q–N1; 3 QxR!, QxQ;
4 R–K8 mate.

Finally, if 1 . . . Q–N1; 2 P–N6, R–B3; 3 Q–Q7 (threatening mate
by 4 R–K8ch etc. or 4 Q–K8ch etc., and also threatening 4 QxB for
good measure), K–B1; 5 Q–K7ch and White mates in two more moves.

| 1 | . . . . | Q–KB1 |
| 2 | Q–K3 | Resigns |

Black is helpless against the threatened 3 R–K8. A notable triumph for White on the last rank.

IVKOV–ELISKASES
Yugoslavia–Austria, 1959

BLACK

WHITE

17. White to play

(See Diagram 18 on page 133)

White's position is clearly preferable, but who would expect him to win right off?

| 1 | B–N6! | Resigns |

Black's Queen is attacked, of course—but in moving his Bishop, White has opened up the ghastly threat of 2 Q–R6 mate. So Black is left without an adequate defense.

BENKO–FUESTER
Portoroz, 1958

BLACK

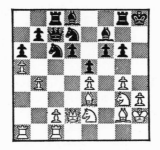

WHITE

18. White to play

SPASSKY–GHITESCU
USSR–Rumania, 1958

BLACK

WHITE

19. White to play

(*See Diagram 19 on page 133*)

White wins by a neat stratagem that has many applications. His objective: queening his passed Pawn.

1	Q–N8ch!	QxQ
2	BxQch	KxB
3	P–B7	Resigns

Black cannot stop the terrible Pawn from advancing, as 3 . . . R–K1 or 3 . . . R–QB5 proves useless when White plays his Rook to Queen 8 in reply.

PAVELCZAK–AMATEUR
Berlin, 1951

BLACK

WHITE

20. White to play

With White's pieces massed threateningly and with Black's Queen far from the scene of action, we are justified in expecting fireworks. The finish is very fine:

1	RxB!	RxR
2	Q–N6ch!!	RxQ
3	PxRch	K–R1
4	N–B7 mate	

(*See Diagram 21 on page 135*)

Black's winning procedure starts off prosaically but flares up brilliantly toward the close.

KAMMINIK–SIMKIN
1959

BLACK

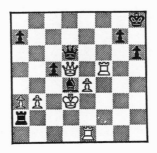

WHITE

21. Black to play

1	....	Q–N6ch
2	K–B4	R–QB7ch
3	K–N5	Q–N1ch
4	K–R4	....

Or 4 K–R5, Q–N3ch; 5 K–R4, Q–R3 mate.

4	....	P–R3

Threatening . . . Q–N4 mate. There is also another threat.

5	Q–B6	....

Or 5 P–N4, Q–N4ch; 6 K–N3, R–QN7 mate.

5	....	Q–N5ch!!

A lovely finish.

6	PxQ	R–QR7 mate

(*See Diagram 22 on page 136*)

Black is satisfied that his Bishop is immune from capture, but he is wrong. White has seen much more deeply into the position.

SCHMIDT–SCHULZ
Prague, 1938

BLACK

WHITE

22. *White to play*

1	QxB!!	RxPch

Of course.

2	QxR	NxR
3	RxPch!!	. . . .

The countercombination. If now 3 . . . RxR; 4 N–B6ch and 5 NxQ when White remains a piece ahead!

3	. . . .	KxR
4	R–N1ch	K–R1

4 . . . K–B1 leads to the same result, while 4 . . . K–R2?? actually leads to mate (5 N–B6ch etc.).

5	RxRch	KxR
6	N–B6ch	Resigns

For 7 NxQ leaves White a piece to the good. A sardonic reminder that in chess as in life we can always expect the unexpected.

(*See Diagram 23 on page* 137)

White has sacrificed the Exchange—and for what?

GILG–ORBACH
Breslau, 1925

BLACK

WHITE

23. *White to play*

1	R–KN1!!	QxR

On 1 . . . Q–B2 or 1 . . . QR1 White has 2 Q–R6 mate.

2	N–N5ch	QxN

He has no choice (if 2 . . . K–R1; 3 Q–R6ch and mate next move).
On the other hand, if 2 . . . K–N2; 3 QxNch, K–N3; 4 Q–R7ch,
K–B3; 5 N–K4 mate.

3	PxQ	Resigns

For if 3 . . . QR–Q1; 4 Q–R6ch, K–N1; 5 P–N6, N–B3; 6 P–N7,
R–B2 (to protect his Knight); 7 Q–R8 mate. A crisp finish.

(*See Diagram 24 on page 138*)

One little Pawn push from White and Black's game caves in.

1	P–Q6!	BxP

Black has no choice; but now his King-side is fatally smashed up.

2	BxN	PxB
3	N–R5!	Resigns

White threatens to force mate by 4 Q–N4ch etc. He also threatens
to win the Queen by 4 NxPch. If 3 . . . K–R1; 4 NxP, Q–N2; 5
Q–R5, K–N2; 6 Q–N5ch, K–R1; 7 Q–R6 and Black cannot stop the
mate.

MIESES–WIARDA
Bad Schandau, 1927

BLACK

WHITE

24. White to play

NIMZOVICH–RUBINSTEIN
Berlin, 1928

BLACK

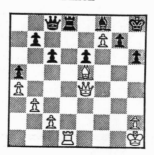

WHITE

25. White to play

(*See Diagram 25 on page 138*)

White wants to play Q–N6 threatening QxRP mate. But this would leave his Rook unprotected, so it seems natural to interpolate 1 RxR, QxR. But then on 2 Q–N6? Black has 2 . . . Q–Q8ch; 3 K–N2, Q–Q4ch followed by . . . QxB. The right way is surprising but simple and effective:

　　　　　1　Q–N6!　　　　　Resigns

For after 1 . . . RxRch; 2 K–N2 Black has only a harmless check or two, after which he must succumb to the threat of QxRP mate.

FINK–KAPPER
Graz, 1932

BLACK

WHITE

26. *White to play*

White has sacrificed two pieces to get this position. Now, for good measure, he sacrifices both Rooks.

　　　　　1　R–B8ch!!　　　　　BxR

If 1 . . . K–B2; 2 Q–B8 mate.

　　　　　2　RxPch!!　　　　　QxR

If 1 . . . K–B2; 2 R–Q7ch forces mate.

　　　　　3　B–N6 mate

Now we see the point of White's first move: Black cannot play . . . K–K1.

PODGORNY–OLEXA
Bratislava, 1948

BLACK

WHITE

27. White to play

White's advantage is overwhelming. If he can be said to have a problem, it is this: What is the very quickest way for him to win? He has a neat solution.

1	N–K7ch	K–B1
2	B–R6ch	K–K1

Now comes the stinger:

3	B–N7!	. . . .

Black finds himself in a queer dilemma. He must capture the Bishop in order to avoid the loss of a piece. But after White's reply he threatens to get a new Queen.

3	. . . .	BxB
4	PxB	KxN

Forced, but now disaster breaks in.

5	Q–N5ch	Resigns

White has a quick mate.

(*See Diagram 28 on page 141*)

Many a player handling the White pieces in this position would resign, for it is "obvious" that White cannot stop one of the Pawns

RICHTER–DOERNTE
Berlin, 1939

BLACK

WHITE

28. *White to play*

from queening. While it is true that White cannot hold back the
Pawns, the fact remains that he has a subtle, astounding win!

| 1 | K–Q6!! | P–Q7 |
| 2 | K–B7! | P–Q8/Q |

What now?

3	R–QR6ch!!	PxR
4	P–N6ch	K–R1
5	P–N7ch	K–R2
6	P–N8/Q mate	

Truly a case of snatching victory from the jaws of defeat.

(*See Diagram 29 on page 142*)

White threatens a three-move mate—but it is Black's turn to play,
and he has a beautiful forced mate:

1	. . . .	RxNch!
2	KxR	R–R8ch!
3	KxR	Q–R5ch

Now watch Black force checkmate despite his enormous material
inferiority.

WESTLER–KREJCIK
Vienna, 1913

BLACK

WHITE

29. Black to play

4	K–N1	Q–R7ch
5	K–B1	Q–R8ch
6	K–Q2	QxPch
7	K–Q3	Q–QB7ch
8	K–Q4	Q–B5ch
9	K–K5	Q–Q4ch
10	K–B6	Q–B2ch
11	K–K5	. . . .

There is a droll alternative in 11 K–N5, Q–B4ch; 12 K–R4, Q–R4 mate.

11	. . . .	Q–B4ch
12	K–Q4	P–B4ch
13	K–B3	Q–QB7 mate

A splendid finish.

GLIGORICH–FOLTYS
Spindleruv Mlyn, 1948

BLACK

WHITE

30. Black to play

UHLMANN–DARGA
Hastings, 1959

BLACK

WHITE

31. White to play

(*See Diagram 30 on page 143*)

A fine example of incisive, perfectly timed play:

1	. . . .	RxN!

All of White's moves are forced.

2	PxR	B–B4ch
3	K–R1	. . . .

Or 3 R–B2, Q–K8ch and Black mates next move.

3	. . . .	BxR
4	NxB	Q–Q5!
	Resigns	

White has no good reply to the mate threat.

(*See Diagram 31 on page 143*)

Surely, you would say, a resignable position for White. Black's pin on the White Rook *must* be decisive. Yet White takes the carefree attitude that pins are made only to be broken, and why?

Well, note the powerful diagonals of the White Bishops. And note that far-advanced White Pawn on King 6. Finally, do you see the connection between this powerful passed Pawn and the diagonal of White's Bishop at Queen Rook 2? The great Nimzovich often spoke about the passed Pawn's "lust to expand." Here we have a notable case in point:

1	RxR!	. . . .

After all the portentous hints this is no longer a great surprise. However, let's follow through the consequence of 1 . . . BxQ; 2 RxRch, NxR; 3 RxNch! (an exquisite sequel), QxR; 4 P–K7 dis ch and White forces mate.

1	. . . .	RxR

Surely this looks reasonably safe and solid.

2	RxR!	Resigns

What a tableau! If 2 . . . QxR; 3 P–K7 dis ch with immediate disaster for Black. Or 2 . . . BxQ; 3 RxN! (threatens mayhem with R–B8ch etc.), B–R3; 4 R–B7!! forcing Black's Queen to give up the blockade (4 . . . QxR; 5 P–K7 dis ch).

And after all these explanations, the mighty passed Pawn has not even moved! Its mere threat to move was enough to destroy Black.

MUELLER–PALDA
Vienna, 1948

BLACK

WHITE

32. Black to play

There is nothing very remarkable about this position, nor is Black's winning procedure particularly flashy. Yet there is a lot to be learned from Black's workmanlike winning method. His Rook on the seventh, pinning White's Knight, will of course spearhead the attack.

      1 . . . .   B–B6!

This beautiful and unexpected move takes advantage of the pin on White's Knight. White must of course capture.

      2 BxB   NxB

Double attack on White's pinned Knight. Again his reply is forced.

      3 R–K1   RxP

The win of a Pawn is the direct consequence of Black's forcing play.

      4 K–K3   . . . .

Black can force a won King and Pawn ending in any event.

      4 . . . .   RxNch

White resigns, for after 5 RxR, NxR; 6 KxN, K–K3; 7 K–K3, K–Q4; 8 K–Q3, P–QR4 Black wins easily. He advances his Queen Knight Pawn and obtains an outside passed Pawn on the Queen-side. This keeps White's King busy on the Queen-side, allowing the successful invasion via . . . K–K5–B6 by Black's King.

HEUSER–KAULING
Cologne, 1960

BLACK

WHITE

33. Black to play

While there is nothing brilliant about Black's play, his winning method is nevertheless appealing.

1 . . . .   Q–KB6ch

This leaves White no choice, as on 2 K–N1 the reply 2 . . . B–K6ch is murderous.

2 Q–B2   Q–R8ch
3 Q–N1   Q–R6ch

Winning a piece, as 4 K–B2 allows 4 . . . B–K6ch.

4 Q–N2   QxQch
5 KxQ   R–K7ch and wins

Black continues 6 . . . RxB. The zigzag checks form an attractive pattern.

HORVATH–SZILADVY
Budapest, 1959

BLACK

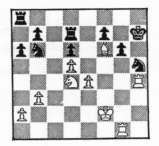

WHITE

34. *White to play*

KUPPER–OLAFSSON
Zurich, 1959

BLACK

WHITE

35. *White to play*

(*See Diagram 34 on page 147*)

The theme is a familiar one, but White's execution in the absence of the Queens lends added interest:

1	RxNch!	PxR
2	R–N7ch	K–R1

But not 2 . . . K–R3; 3 N–B5 mate.

	3 N–B5!	Resigns

Black has no recourse against the quiet Knight move, with its threat of 4 R–N6 dis ch, K–R2; 5 R–R6ch, K–N1; 6 R–R8 mate.

(*See Diagram 35 on page 147*)

White's first shrewd blow topples the hostile position:

1	RxPch!	K–N1

If 1 . . . RxR; 2 N–K6ch wins the Black Queen.

2	R–N7ch!	K–R1

For if 2 . . . KxR; 3 N–K6ch still wins Black's Queen, or if 2 . . . NxR; 3 QxP mate.

3	RxPch	K–N1
4	R–N7ch!	Resigns

For after 4 . . . K–R1; 5 RxP, N(Q2)–B3; 6 R–KB1, Black's position is helpless and hopeless.

PAOLI–SMYSLOV
Venice, 1950

BLACK

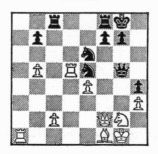

WHITE

36. Black to play and win

(See Diagram 36 on page 148)

Black wins with a crisply calculated sequence:

    1 . . . .   RxP!

If now 2 RxN, QxR, Black comes out the Exchange ahead.

Or if 2 Q–K3, RxNch! winning the Queen—with the same result after 2 Q–Q4 (or 2 Q–K1), N–B6ch etc.

    2 QxR   N–B6ch

And now if 3 K–R1, Q–N6; 4 N moves, Q–N8 mate.

    3 K–B2   Q–N6ch

White resigns, as he must lose his Queen by a discovered check or forking check.

BUCHER–MUELLER
Basle, 1959

BLACK

WHITE

37. White to play

Seemingly White must try his luck in the ending with 1 QxQch etc. Instead, he has an astounding win:

    1 R–QB4ch!!   KxR

Or 1 . . . K–Q3; 2 Q–Q8 mate.

    2 Q–B3 mate

An unexpected knockout. This finish inspired the problem shown in Diagram 8 on page 96.

RICHTER–MROSS
Berlin, 1938

BLACK

WHITE

38. White to play

KERES–GLIGORICH
Zurich, 1959

BLACK

WHITE

39. White to play

(See Diagram 38 on page 150)

White's advanced Pawn is so formidable that White can even offer his Queen:

1	BxB!	RxB

If 1 . . . PxQ; 2 P–N7ch, K–N1; 3 B–Q5ch and mate follows. Or 1 . . . PxB; 2 P–N7ch, K–N1; 3 R–B8ch! forcing mate.

2	QxP	Q–K1
3	P–N7ch	K–N1
4	QxN!	Resigns

If 4 . . . QxQ; 5 R–B8ch forces mate. (4 Q–Q5ch was another way to win.) The White Pawn wedge at King Knight 7 was crushing.

(See Diagram 39 on page 150)

White's brilliant and far-reaching combination is all the more surprising as he can win the Exchange by 1 N–R6ch, K–R1; 2 N–B7ch etc.

1	RxN!	PxR
2	B–N3ch	K–R1
3	NxBP!!	. . . .

Threatens 4 QxRP mate.

3	. . . .	RxN
4	N–N5	. . . .

Renewing the threat. Black is desperate, as he is unable to play . . . N–B1 because of the resulting loss of his Queen.

4	. . . .	RxPch!?
5	K–N1!	. . . .

The simplest.

5	. . . .	R–B8ch!?
6	K–R2!	Resigns

(See Diagram 40 on page 152)

White's control of the open King Bishop file proves deadly:

1	R–B7!!	KxR
2	QxRPch	N–N2

Or 2 . . . K–B1; 3 R–KB1ch, B–B4; 4 N–K6 mate.

3	R–KB1ch	B–B4
4	RxBch!	Resigns

A delightful finish. If 4 . . . PxR; 5 P–N6ch, K–B1; 6 Q–R8 mate.

NACHT–TROIANESCU
Bucharest, 1960

BLACK

WHITE

40. White to play

SAEMISCH–AHUES
Hamburg, 1946

BLACK

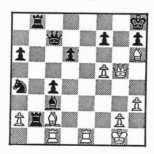

WHITE

41. White to play and win

(See Diagram 41 on page 152)

White wins with one of the most exquisite moves ever played in a game of chess:

       1 R–K5!!   Resigns

For if 1 . . . PxR; 2 Q–N7 mate; or 1 . . . BxR; 2 P–B6, R–N1; 3 B–N7ch and mate next move; or 1 . . . R–KN1; 2 QxRch, KxR; 3 R–K8 mate.

Query: why doesn't 1 P–B6 win without any frills? Because then 1 . . . Q–B4ch! forces the exchange of Queens. This explains White's splendid Rook move.

SIANOVSKY–POGREBISSKY
Kiev, 1955

BLACK

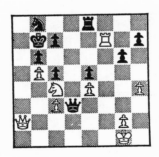

WHITE

42. White to play and win

On a cursory glance, it would seem that both sides have chances. White's continuation comes like a sudden thunderclap:

       1   Q–R7ch!!   KxQ

       2   RxBPch   K–R1

       3   NxNP mate

Black never knew what hit him.

"He hopes to win by pinning."

Brief Candles

Brief they are, and witty and instructive too.

What better way to learn how to play good chess and how to profit by the mistakes of others than by studying these pithy and thought-provoking gamelets?

But if you want to be carefree and prefer not to study, these games are still worth your while. Each of these games sparkles and scintillates. No mistake goes unpunished. The punishment, in fact, always fits the crime.

Such brief games, with their quick, satisfying endings, show us chess in its ideal form. What happens, in effect, is that one player commits a gross mistake and his opponent punishes it incisively. In "real life," alas, this opportunity is often missed. So, here we may say complacently, we get the best of both worlds, and masterly play shines forth like a good deed in a naughty world.

ORDER AND DISORDER

GIUOCO PIANO

Berlin, 1837

	WHITE (*Horwitz*)	BLACK (*Bledow*)
1	P–K4	P–K4
2	N–KB3	N–QB3
3	B–B4	B–B4
4	P–B3	B–N3
5	P–Q4	Q–K2
6	P–Q5?	N–Q1

	7	B–K2?	P–Q3
	8	P–KR3?	P–KB4

White's last three moves make very little sense. Black, on the other hand, goes ahead purposefully with the opening of the King Bishop file.

	9	B–KN5	N–KB3
	10	QN–Q2	Castles
	11	N–R4?	. . . .

He should castle into comparative safety.

	11	. . . .	PxP!
	12	NxP	. . . .

BLACK

WHITE

Position after 12 NxP

	12	. . . .	NxN!

A gilt-edged investment rather than a sacrifice.

	13	BxQ	BxPch
	14	K–B1	N–N6 mate

DOUBLE-BARRELED SHOOTING

PHILIDOR'S DEFENSE

London, 1860

WHITE (*Schulder*) BLACK (*Boden*)

1	P–K4	P–K4
2	N–KB3	P–Q3
3	P–B3	. . . .

Molasses in January. 3 P–Q4! is the move.

3	. . . .	P–KB4!
4	B–B4	N–KB3
5	P–Q4	BPxP
6	PxP	PxN
7	PxN	QxP
8	PxP	N–B3

Thanks to White's feeble play, Black has acquired a fine initiative.

9	P–B4	B–Q2
10	B–K3	Castles
11	N–Q2	R–K1!
12	Q–B3	B–B4!

Black sets a deep trap.

13	Castles/Q?	. . . .

Loses a piece at least. But his game was beyond salvation.

BLACK

WHITE

Position after 13 Castles/Q?

13	. . . .	P–Q4!
14	BxP	QxPch!!
15	PxQ	B–QR6 mate

Played in the springtime of the chess world.

DAMN THE TORPEDOES!

KING's BISHOP's GAMBIT

Posen, 1865

WHITE (*Kornfeld*) BLACK (*Zukertort*)

1	P–K4	P–K4
2	P–KB4	PxP
3	B–QB4	P–Q4
4	BxP	N–KB3
5	N–QB3	B–QN5
6	KN–K2	. . . .

6 N–KB3 is stronger.

6	. . . .	P–B3
7	B–N3	B–N5
8	P–Q3?	. . . .

He should have castled while he still had the opportunity.

BLACK

WHITE

Position after 8 P–Q3?

	8	NxP!
	9 PxN	. . . .

Succumbing to the inevitable, for after 9 Castles, BxQN, White's position is resignable (10 PxB, NxP—or 10 PxN, QxQ; 11 RxQ, BxN).

	9	Q–R5ch
	10 K–B1	P–B6!

Black plays the finish with great energy.

	11 PxP	B–KR6ch
	12 K–N1	B–QB4ch
	13 N–Q4	BxNch
	14 QxB	Q–K8 mate

MY KINGDOM FOR A HORSE

Bishop's Opening

Vienna, 1872

WHITE (*Schlemm*) BLACK (*Wraney*)

	1 P–K4	P–K4
	2 B–B4	N–KB3
	3 N–KB3	NxP
	4 P–Q4	PxP
	5 QxP	N–B4

5 . . . N–KB3 gives a better development.

	6 Castles	N–K3
	7 N–K5!?	. . . .

This Queen sacrifice is only the preliminary to the real point. (*See Diagram on page 160*)

	7	NxQ?
	8 BxPch	K–K2
	9 B–KN5ch	K–Q3
	10 N–B4ch	K–B3
	11 BxQ	NxP?

This is the move White has been waiting for.

	12 R–B1	NxR
	13 N–K5 dbl ch	. . . .

Position after 7 N–K5!?

White has a terrific attack.

         13 . . . .   K–N3

After 13 . . . K–Q3 White still has a mating attack with 14 BxPch, K–K2; 15 N–QB3!, K–B3; 16 N–Q5ch etc.

         14 RxP   P–Q3

He should try . . . K–R3.

         15 R–B6 dbl ch   K–N4

         16 N–QB3ch   K–N5

         17 P–QR3 mate

SORCERER'S APPRENTICE

KING'S BISHOP'S GAMBIT

Breslau, 1876

WHITE (*Riemann*) BLACK (*Anderssen*)

1	P–K4	P–K4
2	P–KB4	PxP
3	B–B4	Q–R5ch
4	K–B1	P–Q4
5	BxP	N–KB3
6	N–QB3	B–QN5
7	P–K5?	. . . .

This gives Black the initiative. At that time Riemann was a school-boy disciple of the great Anderssen.

7	. . . .	BxN
8	PxN	BxBP
9	N–B3	Q–R4
10	Q–K2ch	K–Q1
11	Q–B4	R–K1!

Setting a neat trap which every schoolboy ought to know enough to avoid.

12	BxP??	. . . .

BLACK

WHITE

Position after 12 BxP??

12	. . . .	QxNch!

Black has a forced mate.

13	PxQ	B–R6ch
14	K–B2	B–R5ch
15	K–N1	R–K8ch
16	Q–B1	RxQ mate

KIND HEARTS AND CORONETS

Jerome Gambit

London, 1880

	WHITE (*Amateur*)	BLACK (*Blackburne*)
1	P–K4	P–K4
2	N–KB3	N–QB3
3	B–B4	B–B4
4	BxPch?	KxB
5	NxPch	NxN

For an amateur to play this absurd gambit against a Blackburne is a spectacle for the gods. But the great master is in a sporting mood and turns the game into a little gem.

6	Q–R5ch	P–KN3!?
7	QxN	P–Q3!?
8	QxR	Q–R5
9	Castles	N–B3

Now Blackburne is fully at home in a situation where *he* is doing the attacking and sacrificing.

| 10 | P–QB3 | . . . . |

Or 10 P–KN3, Q–R6 and White is helpless against 11 . . . N–N5.

10	. . . .	N–N5
11	P–KR3	BxPch
12	K–R1	. . . .

BLACK

WHITE

Position after 12 *K–R1*

12	. . . .	B–KB4!

White is being killed with kindness.

13	QxR	QxPch!
14	PxQ	BxP mate

COFFEEHOUSE STYLE

Bishop's Opening

New York, 1887

WHITE (*Richardson*) BLACK (*Delmar*)

1	P–K4	P–K4
2	B–QB4	N–KB3
3	N–KB3	NxP
4	N–B3	NxP?

Just for fun.

5	KxN	B–B4ch
6	P–Q4	PxP
7	R–K1ch	K–B1

The attack has already passed to White.

8	N–K4	B–N3
9	Q–Q3!	. . . .

White is hatching a sublime combination.

9	. . . .	P–Q4
10	Q–R3ch	K–N1
11	BxP	QxB

(*See Diagram on page 164*)

12	N–B6ch!	PxN
13	Q–B8ch!	KxQ
14	B–R6ch	K–N1
15	R–K8 mate	

BLACK

WHITE

Position after 11 . . . QxB

DISCOVERING A DIAGONAL

Giuoco Piano

New York, 1894

WHITE (*Albin*)   BLACK (*Shipley*)

1	P–K4	P–K4
2	N–KB3	N–QB3
3	B–B4	B–B4
4	Castles	N–B3
5	P–B3	Castles

A flabby reply that allows White a tremendous initiative in the center. 5 . . . NxP was much better.

6	P–Q4	PxP
7	PxP	B–N3
8	P–Q5	N–K2
9	P–K5	N–K1

See the previous note. Black's position is bleak indeed.

10	P–Q6	PxP
11	PxP	N–N3
12	B–KN5	N–B3
13	N–B3	P–KR3

Black hastens to drive off the pinning Bishop before White has time for N–Q5 breaking up Black's King-side Pawns. But White has a crafty interpolation.

| 14 | Q–Q3! | PxB |
| 15 | QxN | N–R2 |

Otherwise NxP is deadly. Now comes a stunning surprise.

BLACK

WHITE

Position after 15 . . . N–R2

| 16 | N–Q5!! | . . . . |

This threatens 17 N–K7ch, K–R1; 18 NxP and wins.

16	. . . .	PxQ
17	N–K7 dbl ch	K–R1
18	N/K7xP mate	

A startling finish.

CLASSIC THEME

FRENCH DEFENSE

Vienna, 1894

WHITE (*Schlechter*)	BLACK (*Wolf*)
1 P–K4	P–K3
2 P–Q4	P–Q4
3 N–QB3	N–KB3
4 B–KN5	B–K2

5	BxN	BxB
6	N–B3	Castles
7	P–K5	B–K2
8	B–Q3	B–Q2?

Too passive. Counteraction against White's center (8 . . . P–QB4!)
is more to the point.

9	P–KR4!	P–KB3

BLACK

WHITE

Position after 9 . . . P–KB3

10	N–KN5!	PxN?

The only chance to keep his head above water was 10 . . . P–KB4!

11	BxPch!	. . . .

The classic theme.

11	. . . .	KxB
12	PxP dis ch	K–N1
13	R–R8ch!	. . . .

Triumph of the open Rook file.

13	. . . .	K–B2

Or 13 . . . KxR; 14 Q–R5ch, K–N1; 15 P–N6 and White forces
mate.

14	Q–R5ch	P–KN3
15	Q–R7ch	K–K1
16	QxP mate	

Slick attacking play by White.

HIGH VOLTAGE

Ruy Lopez

Scheveningen, 1905

	WHITE (*Leonhardt*)	BLACK (*Esser*)
1	P–K4	P–K4
2	N–KB3	N–QB3
3	B–N5	N–B3
4	Castles	NxP
5	P–Q4	N–Q3
6	B–R4	. . . .

An alternative gambit is 6 PxP!?, NxB; 7 P–QR4 recovering the piece with a good attack.

6	. . . .	P–K5
7	N–K5	B–K2
8	N–QB3	Castles
9	P–B4	P–B3

A plausible attempt to get rid of the intrusive White Knight.

10	B–N3ch	K–R1

BLACK

WHITE

Position after 10 . . . K–R1

11	N–N6ch!	PxN
12	P–B5	NxBP

What else? White was threatening 13 PxP followed by 14 Q–R5 mate.

13	RxN!	P–Q4

Of course not 13 . . . PxR; 14 Q–R5 mate.

   14 R–R5ch!   K–N1

For 14 . . . PxR; 15 QxPch, K–N1; 16 BxPch is disastrous for him.

   15 RxP!   Q–K1
   16 R–Q8 dis ch Resigns

White played with heart-warming energy.

HEADLESS HORSEMEN

FOUR KNIGHTS' GAME

Prague, 1908

WHITE (*Abonyi*) BLACK (*Hromadka*)

1	P–K4	P–K4
2	N–KB3	N–QB3
3	N–B3	N–B3
4	B–N5	N–Q5
5	B–R4	P–B3
6	Castles	B–B4

So far White has fought the temptation to capture the King Pawn —a time-consuming enterprise.

7	NxP	P–Q3
8	N–Q3	B–KN5!
9	Q–K1	. . . .

(See Diagram on page 169)

   9 . . . .   N–B6ch!

This sacrifice is fully justified by the unwieldiness of White's pieces.

10	PxN	QBxP
11	P–K5	Castles!

For if 12 PxN, QxP, White is helpless against the threat of . . . Q–N3 mate or . . . Q–N4 mate.

   12 PxP   N–N5

Threatens . . . Q–R5 followed by mate.

   13 Q–K7   BxQP
      Resigns

For if 14 QxQ, BxP mate. A nice touch.

BLACK

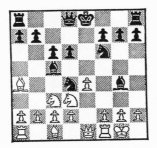

WHITE

Position after 9 Q–K1

APPETITE GROWS WITH EATING

KING'S KNIGHT'S OPENING

Paris, 1913

WHITE (*Rodzynski*) BLACK (*Alekhine*)

1	P–K4	P–K4
2	N–KB3	N–QB3
3	B–B4	P–Q3
4	P–B3	B–N5
5	Q–N3	Q–Q2
6	N–N5	. . . .

Rightly dismissing 6 QxP, R–N1; 7 Q–R6, White prepares the capture in what he expects will be a more advantageous form.

6	. . . .	N–R3
7	BxPch	NxB
8	NxN	QxN
9	QxP	K–Q2!

This sacrifice of the Exchange is part of a deep plan.

10	QxR	Q–B5!

Threatens . . . Q–K7 mate.

11	P–B3	. . . .

BLACK

WHITE

Position after 11 P–B3

| 11 | .... | BxP! |

With White's Queen out of play—and on a vulnerable spot at that—Black can indulge in a very beautiful combination.

| 12 | PxB | N–Q5! |

To this there is no better reply than 13 PxN, allowing Black to recover all his sacrificed material with a winning position.

13	P–Q3	QxQP
14	PxN	B–K2!
15	QxR	B–R5 mate

A little essay on chess tactics.

WHITE STOOPS TO CONQUER

Center Counter Game

Scheveningen, 1913

WHITE (*Lasker*)	BLACK (*Mieses*)
1 P–K4	P–Q4
2 PxP	N–KB3
3 P–Q4	QxP
4 N–QB3	Q–QR4
5 N–B3	B–B4
6 N–K5	N–K5
7 Q–B3!	N–Q3

The plausible 7 . . . P–K3? allows 8 N–B4!, Q–N5; 9 P–QR3 and Black is lost.

$$8 \quad \text{B–Q2} \qquad \dots$$

Threatening to win with 9 N–Q5!

8	. . . .	P–K3
9	P–KN4!	B–N3
10	P–KR4!	Q–N3

BLACK

WHITE

Position after 10 . . . Q–N3

11 Castles!   P–KB3

Black must provide against P–R5 and is thereby forced to create a fatal Pawn weakness. (This explains White's ninth and tenth moves.) As for 11 . . . QxQP, this loses a piece: 12 NxB, RPxN; 13 B–K3, Q–N5; 14 P–R3, Q–R4; 15 RxN! followed by 16 QxNP etc.

12	NxB	PxN
13	B–Q3	QxQP

Desperation; on 13 . . . K–B2; 14 QR–K1 gives White a winning attack.

14	BxPch	K–Q2
15	B–K3	Q–N5
16	P–QR3!	Q–QB5
17	QxNP	Q–B3
18	B–K4!	Resigns

White wins a Rook. An enchanting game.

FLASH FLOOD

French Defense

London, 1927

WHITE (*Yates*) BLACK (*Censer*)

1	P–K4	P–K3
2	P–Q4	P–Q4
3	N–QB3	PxP

This timid defense allows White to develop a strong initiative.

4	NxP	N–Q2
5	N–KB3	KN–B3
6	N–N3	P–QN3?

Premature. Better 6 . . . P–B4 or else 7 . . . B–K2 with 8 . . . Castles to follow.

7	B–QN5!	B–N2
8	N–K5	B–K2
9	B–B6!	Q–B1
10	N–R5!	Castles
11	BxN	NxB

BLACK

WHITE

Position after 11 . . . NxB

12	B–R6!	. . . .

For if 12 . . . PxB; 13 NxN, QxN; 14 Q–N4ch, B–N4; 15 N–B6ch winning the Black Queen.

12	. . . .	NxN

13 PxN   R–Q1

Or 13 . . . PxB; 14 Q–N4ch, B–N4; 15 P–KR4 with a rapidly decisive attack.

14   Q–N4   P–N3
15   Q–KB4!   P–QB4
16   N–B6ch   K–R1

If 16 . . . BxN; 17 QxB and White forces mate.

17   Q–R4   Resigns

Black has no counter to the threat of 18 B–N7ch!, for if 17 . . . R–KN1; 18 B–B8! wins.

DOUBLE TAKE

Queen's Gambit Declined

Tenby, 1928

WHITE (*Spencer*)   BLACK (*Fairhurst*)

1   P–Q4   P–Q4
2   B–N5   N–KB3
3   N–Q2   B–B4
4   P–QB4   P–K3
5   KN–B3   QN–Q2
6   N–R4   . . . .

White is playing with fire, but he doesn't know it.

6   . . . .   B–K5!
7   PxP   PxP
8   NxB?   . . . .

Who could dream that this capture actually loses a piece? (*See Diagram on page 174*)

8   . . . .   NxN!!
9   BxQ   . . . .

Biting into the sour apple.

9   . . . .   B–N5ch
10   Q–Q2   BxQch
11   K–Q1   RxB
12   P–B3   . . . .

A momentary flicker of hope.

BLACK

WHITE

Position after 8 NxB?

12	....	B–N4!
	Resigns	

Black remains a piece ahead.

TAINTED ROOKS

FRENCH DEFENSE

Aachen, 1943

(Blindfold Exhibition)

WHITE (*Saemisch*) BLACK (*Amateur*)

1	P–K4	P–K3
2	P–Q4	P–Q4
3	N–QB3	B–N5
4	P–K5	P–QB4
5	B–Q2	PxP
6	N–N5	B–B4

As the Bishop doesn't have much of a future, 6 . . . BxBch was preferable.

7	P–QN4	B–N3
8	Q–N4	K–B1
9	N–KB3	N–QB3
10	Q–B4	P–B3

11	PxP	QxP
12	N–B7	BxN

It is poor judgment to allow the penetration by White's Queen.
12 . . . QxQ was decidedly more prudent.

13	QxB	P–KR3
14	P–N5	P–Q6

Not merely attacking the White Rook, but also threatening mate in
two. The blindfold player has a smart reply.

BLACK

WHITE

Position after 14 . . . P–Q6

15	BxQP!	QxRch
16	K–K2	Q–B3

After 16 . . . QxR; 17 PxN the brutal threat of B–N4ch is decisive.
However, even discretion is no longer good enough to save Black.

17	PxN	Q–K2
18	B–N4!!	QxB
19	Q–Q8ch	K–B2
20	N–K5 mate	

A lovely finish.

DOUBLE, DOUBLE, TOIL AND TROUBLE

FRENCH DEFENSE

Warsaw, 1935

WHITE (*Dake*)	BLACK (*Cranston*)
1 P–K4	P–K3
2 P–Q4	P–Q4
3 N–QB3	N–KB3
4 B–KN5	PxP
5 NxP	B–K2
6 BxN	BxB
7 N–KB3	N–Q2

As in the Yates–Censer game (page 172), Black's timid opening line gives White a strong initiative.

8 P–B3	Castles
9 Q–B2	B–K2
10 Castles	. . . .

White plans to force the advance of one of Black's King-side Pawns, after which it should become possible to open a file for attacking purposes.

10	P–QB3
11 P–KR4	N–B3
12 NxNch	BxN
13 B–Q3	P–KN3

Just what White wants, but after 13 . . . P–KR3; 14 P–KN4 White could still carry out his plan.

14 P–R5	K–N2
15 R–R2	R–KN1
16 Q–Q2	K–R1?

By fleeing from the threatened sector (16 . . . K–B1), Black would at least stave off the evil hour.

| 17 Q–R6 | B–N2 |

The stage is set.

(*See Diagram on page 177*)

| 18 QxRPch! | KxQ |
| 19 PxP mate! | |

BLACK

WHITE

Position after 17 . . . B–N2

THE OLD ONE-TWO

Center Game

Vienna, 1936

(Simultaneous Exhibition)

WHITE (*Alekhine*)   BLACK (*Amateur*)

1	P–K4	P–K4
2	P–Q4	P–KB3??

Such "caution" is more damaging than recklessness.

3	PxP	PxP
4	Q–R5ch	K–K2
5	QxKPch	K–B2
6	B–QB4ch	P–Q4
7	BxPch	K–N3
8	Q–N3ch	K–R4
9	B–B7ch	P–KN3
10	P–KR3!	. . . .

Threatening an exquisite finish by 11 Q–N4ch!!, BxQ; 12 PxB dbl ch, KxP; 13 B–K6 mate.

10	. . . .	Q–B3
11	N–KB3	. . . .

Now White threatens 12 Q–N4ch!!, BxQ; 13 PxB dbl ch, KxP; 14 B–K6ch!, QxB; 15 R–R4 mate.

$$11 \quad \ldots \qquad\qquad \text{B–K2}$$

BLACK

WHITE

Position after 11 . . . *B–K2*

White announced mate in 6:

12	Q–N4ch!	BxQ
13	PxB dbl ch	KxP
14	N–R2ch!	K–R4
15	N–B1 dis ch	K–N5
16	B–K6ch!	QxB
17	P–KB3 mate	

Q.E.D.

DANISH PASTRY

DANISH GAMBIT

Detroit, 1945

(Simultaneous Exhibition)

WHITE (*Denker*)   BLACK (*Gonzalez*)

1	P–K4	P–K4
2	P–Q4	PxP
3	P–QB3	PxP

	4	B–QB4	PxP
	5	BxNP	B–N5ch?
	6	K–B1!?	. . . .

Tricky.

	6	. . . .	N–KB3
	7	P–K5	N–N1
	8	Q–N4	B–B1
	9	Q–B3	N–KR3
	10	N–B3	B–K2
	11	N–Q5!	Castles
	12	N–B6ch!	K–R1

But not 12 . . . PxN; 13 PxP, B–Q3; 14 Q–R5 and White has a winning attack.

	13	N–R3	BxN?

He should have tried 13 . . . P–Q3.

	14	PxB	P–KN3
	15	Q–B4!	N–B4

Black has nothing better, for if 15 . . . N–N1; 16 N–N5, Q–K1; 17 R–K1 wins for White.

	16	N–N5	N–Q3

BLACK

WHITE

Position after 16 . . . N–Q3

White now brings off a striking finish.

	17	NxBPch!!	NxN

The alternative was 17 . . . RxN; 18 BxR, NxB; 19 Q–R6!!, Q–N1; 20 R–K1!!, NxQ; 21 P–B7 dis ch, Q–N2; 22 R–K8ch (or 22 P–B8/Qch) and mate follows.

18   Q–R6!!   Resigns

The final moves might have been 18 . . . R–N1 (if 18 . . . NxQ; 19 P–B7 dis ch forces mate); 19 BxN, Q–B1; 20 B–Q5!!, QxQ; 21 P–B7 dis ch forcing mate. A triumph for the long diagonal.

A MODERN "IMMORTAL"

SICILIAN DEFENSE

Bad Gastein, 1948

WHITE (*Rossolimo*) BLACK (*Romanenko*)

1	P–K4	P–QB4
2	N–KB3	N–QB3
3	B–N5	P–KN3
4	Castles	B–N2
5	R–K1	N–B3
6	N–B3	N–Q5

Black overrates this move and consequently finds himself uncomfortably behind in development. 6 . . . P–Q3 was decidedly preferable.

7	P–K5	N–N1
8	P–Q3	NxB
9	NxN	P–QR3

Black thinks of this move as a necessary preliminary to . . . P–Q3. The consequences are hair-raising.

BLACK

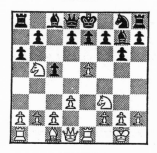

WHITE

Position after 9 . . . P–QR3

10	N–Q6ch!	PxN

The only way to hang on was 10 . . . K–B1, though it would have left Black in a disagreeable situation.

11	B–N5!	Q–R4

There is no good alternative, as 11 . . . N–K2 is answered by 12 PxP with murderous effect, and 11 . . . P–B3; 12 PxBP dis ch, K–B2; 13 PxB is at least as devastating.

12	PxP dis ch	K–B1
13	R–K8ch!	KxR
14	Q–K2ch	K–B1
15	B–K7ch	K–K1
16	B–Q8 dis ch!	KxB
17	N–N5!	Resigns

The real point of White's far-reaching combination is that 17 . . . N–R3 allows 18 Q–K7 mate.

"Spike can't be disturbed now. He's in the middle game."

Chess Fireworks

Though these games are heavyweights in comparison with what you have just seen, they are anything but heavy. With one exception, these games range between twenty-one and thirty moves. They are arranged in chronological order to give you a good picture of how chess has changed—for the better, let us hope—through more than a century of master play.

How were the games selected? A good question, easier asked than answered. In my time I have played over thousands of master games. Of these I would say that perhaps four thousand deserve to be collected in book form—and maybe some day they will. That is to say, one could make a hundred collections without duplicating any of the games. Here is one such collection.

I wouldn't dream of claiming this is the best possible collection. What I can say is that I ransacked my memory for short, pointed, delightfully lively games, and here is the result. Arbitrary? I admit it. Some masters are represented with three games; others don't turn up at all. So? If these games amuse you, pass the time agreeably, make you marvel at the seemingly inexhaustible ingenuity of the great masters, then they have admirably served their purpose.

THE OLD SCHOOL TIE

Daniel Harrwitz was a vain, temperamental master of the old school, complete with colorful chess-motif cuff links.

Evans Gambit

Brighton, 1848

WHITE (*D. Harrwitz*) BLACK (*Allies*)
(Blindfold)

1	P–K4	P–K4
2	N–KB3	N–QB3
3	B–B4	B–B4
4	P–QN4	. . . .

The fashionable opening of the day. Few players were so unchivalrous as to decline the gambit.

4	. . . .	BxNP
5	P–B3	B–B4
6	P–Q4	PxP
7	Castles	P–Q3
8	PxP	B–N3
9	N–B3	KN–K2?

This is asking for trouble.

10	N–KN5	P–Q4

If 10 . . . Castles; 11 Q–R5 and White wins.

11	NxQP	BxP

BLACK

WHITE

Position after 11 . . . BxP

12 NxBP!! . . . .

The most obvious reply, 12 . . . KxN, loses to 13 NxP dis ch, K–B1; 14 Q–B3ch, B–B3 (if 14 . . . B–B4; 15 N–K6ch wins Black's Queen—or 14 . . . N–B4 and 15 B–R3ch is decisive); 15 QxBch!, PxQ; 16 B–KR6 mate.

If 13 . . . K–B3; 14 Q–R5 yields a winning attack—if 14 . . . P–KR3; 15 Q–B7ch, K–K4; 16 Q–B4 mate.

12	. . . .	Q–Q2
13	NxR	BxR
14	Q–R5ch	P–KN3
15	QxRP	N–Q1

White stokes up the attack with another sacrifice:

16	N–B6ch!!	BxN
17	B–B7ch	NxB
18	QxNch	K–Q1
19	Q–B8ch	Q–K1
20	R–Q1ch	N–Q4

The grim alternative is 20 . . . B–Q2; 21 N–B7ch, K–B1; 22 QxQch, BxQ; 23 R–Q8 mate.

21	QxBch	Q–K2
22	RxNch	B–Q2
23	N–B7ch	K–K1
24	R–K5	QxR
25	NxQ	Resigns

MISSPENT YOUTH

In his old age Steinitz was such a fanatical preacher for defensive play that he must have regretted the brilliancies of his youth. Here is one of the most attractive.

CENTER COUNTER GAME

London, 1862

WHITE (*W. Steinitz*) BLACK (*A. Mongredien*)

1	P–K4	P–Q4
2	PxP	QxP
3	N–QB3	Q–Q1?

| 4 | P–Q4 | P–K3? |

Such timid play augurs a bad end for Black.

5	N–B3	N–KB3
6	B–Q3	B–K2
7	Castles	Castles
8	B–K3	P–QN3
9	N–K5	B–N2
10	P–B4	QN–Q2
11	Q–K2	N–Q4

This removal of Black's best defensive piece creates latent dangers.

| 12 | N/B3xN | PxN |
| 13 | R–B3 | P–KB4 |

Plugging up a leak in the dike. (White was threatening to win with 14 BxPch!, KxB; 15 R–R3ch, K–N1; 16 Q–R5.)

| 14 | R–R3 | P–N3 |
| 15 | P–KN4! | PxP? |

Giving White the opportunity for a far-reaching combination. Correct was 15 . . . NxN followed by . . . B–B1.

BLACK

WHITE

Position after 15 . . . PxP?

16	RxP!!	NxN
17	BPxN	KxR
18	QxP	R–KN1

On 18 . . . Q–K1, White wins with 19 Q–R5ch, K–N1; 20 BxP, R–B2; 21 K–R1!, B–KB1; 22 R–KN1, B–N2; 23 B–R6!

Or if 18 . . . R–B4; 19 BxR, PxB; 20 QxPch, K–R1; 21 Q–R5ch followed by 22 K–R1! and the decisive inroad of White's Rook.

19	Q–R5ch	K–N2
20	Q–R6ch!	K–B2
21	Q–R7ch	K–K3

Against 21 . . . R–N2, White has an attractive winning line in 22 BxPch, K–B1; 23 Q–R8ch, R–N1; 24 B–R6 mate.

22	Q–R3ch	K–B2
23	R–KB1ch	K–K1
24	Q–K6	R–N2

Though Black is still a Rook ahead, he is defenseless.

25	B–KN5!!	Q–Q2

Or 25 . . . P–R3; 26 R–B7!!, RxR; 27 BxP and wins.

26	BxPch	RxB
27	QxRch	K–Q1
28	R–B8ch	Q–K1
29	QxQ mate	

The great Morphy had encountered Mongredien twelve times in match play, and always without a brilliancy!

FIREWORKS PAR EXCELLENCE

In the hands of a great attacking player the King's Gambit almost invariably assures fireworks par excellence.

KIESERITZKY GAMBIT

London, 1863

WHITE (*W. Steinitz*) BLACK (*S. Deacon*)

1	P–K4	P–K4
2	P–KB4	PxP
3	N–KB3	P–KN4
4	P–KR4	P–N5
5	N–K5	N–KB3
6	B–B4	P–Q4
7	PxP	B–Q3
8	P–Q4	N–R4

Black seems to have come out of the opening in fine shape.

9	N–QB3	Q–K2
10	B–N5ch	P–QB3

This speculation on winning a piece (Black holds . . . P–B3 in reserve) is nicely refuted. However, if 10 . . . K–Q1; 11 Castles!, BxN; 12 PxB, QxRP (threatens . . . P–N6); 13 RxP!, NxR; 14 BxN, P–N6; 15 Q–B3!, R–N1; 16 P–K6!!, PxP; 17 BxNP!!, Q–N4; 18 Q–B7!, P–K4; 19 QxRch!, QxQ; 20 B–R4ch, Resigns (Steinitz–Belaiev, London, 1866).

11	PxP	PxP

Now Steinitz begins a characteristically deep combination.

12	N–Q5!!	Q–K3

BLACK

WHITE

Position after 12 . . . *Q–K3*

13	N–B7ch!!	BxN
14	B–B4	Q–K2
15	BxPch	K–B1
16	BxN	BxN
17	PxB	QxPch
18	Q–K2!!	QxB

Black forlornly realizes that while 18 . . . QxQch etc. breaks the attack, it leads to a lost ending.

19	BxP	B–B4
20	Castles/K	N–Q2
21	B–R6ch!	K–B2

In the event of 21 . . . K–N1 there follows 22 Q–B4ch, Q–B2; 23 Q–B3!, Q–N3; 24 RxB, QxB; 25 Q–B4ch leading to mate.

22	RxBch!	QxR
23	R–KB1	QxRch

24	QxQch	K–N3
25	B–N5!	P–KR3
26	Q–Q3ch!	Resigns

For if 26 . . . K–R4; 27 Q–B5 forces mate. One of the finest games ever played with the King's Gambit.

THE OLD AND THE NEW

Tchigorin's style had many paradoxical features. Although he pioneered some of the basic aspects of modern chess, he was firmly anchored in the old-fashioned, mid-nineteenth-century style of Morphy's contemporaries.

SCOTCH GAME

Match, 1880

WHITE (*M. Tchigorin*) BLACK (*E. Schiffers*)

1	P–K4	P–K4
2	N–KB3	N–QB3
3	P–Q4	. . . .

Once exceedingly popular, this opening turns up very rarely nowadays.

3	. . . .	PxP
4	NxP	B–B4
5	B–K3	Q–B3
6	P–QB3	KN–K2
7	B–QB4	P–Q3
8	P–B4	. . . .

A promising Pawn sacrifice, typical of the strongly speculative cast of Tchigorin's thinking.

8	. . . .	Q–N3
9	Castles	QxP
10	R–K1	Q–N3
11	NxN	BxBch
12	RxB	PxN
13	Q–K2	Q–B3

As Black finds himself under heavy pressure on the King file, he should have returned the Pawn with 13 . . . B–K3 etc.

14	N–Q2	P–Q4
15	B–Q3	B–K3
16	R–KB1!	P–N3

But not 16 . . . Castles/K?; 17 P–B5 and White wins a piece.

17	N–N3	Castles/K
18	P–N4!	. . . .

Black is by no means out of the woods, as White has renewed the troublesome threat of P–B5. For example, 18 . . . Q–R5? loses a piece after 19 P–B5. Black's best seems to be 18 . . . KR–K1.

18	. . . .	QR–K1
19	N–B5	. . . .

Now 19 . . . Q–R5? still will not do because of 20 P–B5, PxP; 21 PxP, B–B1; 22 P–B6 and White wins a piece.

19	. . . .	P–Q5
20	P–N5!	Q–R1

Not very inviting, but 20 . . . Q–N2; 21 RxB, PxR; 22 NxKP, Q–B2; 23 NxR, KxN; 24 PxP distinctly favors White.

BLACK

WHITE

Position after 20 . . . Q–R1

21	RxB!	PxR
22	QxPch	K–N2

After 22 . . . R–B2; 23 B–B4, Q–N2; 24 N–Q7, White wins.

23	R–K1!	PxP

There is no way out for Black. On 23 . . . Q–N1; 24 Q–K5ch forces mate. Nor would 23 . . . R–B2 help because of 24 B–B4, QR–KB1; 25 QxN! etc.

| 24 | QxNch! | RxQ |
| 25 | RxRch | Resigns |

White mates prettily in three more moves. A game played with the famous Tchigorin verve.

CHANGE OF PACE

We think respectfully of Siegbert Tarrasch as the grave, profound systematizer of modern positional chess. But when he was in the mood he could play a gambit with the best of them.

EVANS GAMBIT

Nuremberg, 1889

WHITE (*S. Tarrasch*)   BLACK (*C. Kelz*)

1	P–K4	P–K4
2	N–KB3	N–QB3
3	B–B4	B–B4
4	P–QN4	BxNP
5	P–B3	B–R4
6	P–Q4	PxP
7	Castles	PxP

The ominously named Compromised Defense, theoretically feasible but perhaps too difficult for practical play.

8	Q–N3	Q–B3
9	P–K5	Q–N3
10	NxP	KN–K2
11	B–R3	QR–N1

A more judicious alternative is 11 . . . P–N4 returning some of his booty for a breath of fresh air.

12	N–Q5!	NxN
13	BxN	P–N4
14	P–K6!	. . . .

Tarrasch cleverly opens up new avenues of attack and at the same time devalues Black's Pawn position to a point where the material advantage is worthless.

| 14 | . . . . | BPxP |

15	BxN!	PxB
16	N–K5!	. . . .

This Knight is destined to work wonders.

16	. . . .	Q–K5
17	Q–N3!	P–N3

Black will have to pay a heavy price for this weakening of the long diagonal; but 17 . . . R–N1 will not do because of 18 Q–N5, P–N5; 19 QR–Q1, B–R3; 20 R–Q7 winning.

18	Q–N5	P–N5
19	QR–Q1!	Castles
20	B–N2	R–N4

Black sets a pretty trap. If 21 N–N4?!, Black does not respond 21 . . . RxQ??, which would allow 22 N–R6 mate. Instead, he has the viciously effective reply 21 . . . QxPch!

BLACK

WHITE

Position after 20 . . . R–N4

21 N–B7!! P–K4

Not 21 . . . RxQ; 22 N–R6 mate. Nor will 21 . . . RxN do because of 22 R–Q8ch, R–B1; 23 Q–B6! Or 21 . . . KxN; 22 Q–B6ch and mate next move.

22 N–R6ch K–R1

If 22 . . . K–N2; 23 Q–K7ch! decides.

23	R–Q8	K–N2
24	RxR	KxR
25	Q–B6ch	K–K1
26	N–N8!	Resigns

Black is helpless against the coming Q–K7 mate. The Evans has lived up to its reputation.

TRAPPER TRAPPED

By an amusing turn of events Tchigorin, the great master of brilliant tactics, falls victim to a sly trap.

RUY LOPEZ

Match, 1893

	WHITE (*S. Tarrasch*)	BLACK (*M. Tchigorin*)
1	P–K4	P–K4
2	N–KB3	N–QB3
3	B–N5	P–QR3
4	B–R4	N–B3
5	N–B3	B–N5

The Bishop has no future here. 5 . . . B–K2 is better.

6	N–Q5	B–R4?
7	Castles	P–QN4
8	B–N3	P–Q3
9	P–Q3	B–KN5
10	P–B3	N–K2?

BLACK

WHITE

Position after 10 . . . N–K2?

11	NxP!!	PxN

Or 11 . . . BxQ; 12 NxNch, K–B1 (avoiding 12 . . . PxN; 13 BxPch, K–B1; 14 B–R6 mate); 13 N–Q7ch and White will be two Pawns up.

12	NxNch	PxN
13	QxB	N–N3

But not 13 . . . QxP??; 14 R–Q1 and Black is lost.

14	B–Q5	QR–N1
15	P–KB4!	P–B3

Black seeks complications. He gets them.

16	BxQBPch	K–K2

Threatens . . . Q–N3ch winning a piece.

17	B–Q5	P–N5
18	PxKP	Q–N3ch
19	K–R1	NxP
20	Q–R5!	. . . .

White is angling for 21 RxP!, QxR (if 21 . . . KxR; 22 Q–N5 mate); 22 B–N5 winning Black's Queen.

20	. . . .	N–N3
21	RxP!!	KxR
22	B–N5ch	K–N2

If 22 . . . K–K4; 23 B–K7 dis ch leads to mate.

23	Q–R6ch	K–N1
24	R–KB1	R–KB1
25	B–KB6	QxB

He has nothing better.

26	RxQ	Resigns

For White threatens 27 RxNch, PxR; 28 QxP mate. Tchigorin generally *won* his games in this style.

POINTED RETORTS

This game is notable for the steely elegance of White's bright attacking play.

GIUOCO PIANO

Berlin, 1902

WHITE (*O. Bernstein*)   BLACK (*O. Piotrovsky*)

	WHITE	BLACK
1	P–K4	P–K4
2	N–KB3	N–QB3
3	B–B4	B–B4
4	P–B3	N–B3
5	P–Q4	PxP
6	Castles!?	. . . .

White offers a Pawn in order to liven up the proceedings.

6	. . . .	NxP
7	PxP	B–N3
8	R–K1	P–Q4
9	BxP	QxB
10	N–B3	Q–KR4
11	RxNch	B–K3

While this does not lose a piece, Black nevertheless is by no means out of the woods.

12	P–Q5	Castles/Q
13	B–N5!	P–B3

If instead 13 . . . R–Q2; 14 Q–N3!, N–R4; 15 PxB! and White gets more than enough material for his Queen.

Or 13 . . . R–Q3; 14 Q–K2!, BxP; 15 R–K8ch, RxR; 16 QxRch, N–Q1; 17 N–N5, R–Q2; 18 N–K5 and White wins.

14	RxB	PxB
15	Q–R4!	N–N1

The rapid unfolding of White's onslaught on Black's castled position is rather surprising.

16	R–QB1	R–Q2
17	RxB!!	RPxR
18	N–K5	R–K2

Now White can win by 19 Q–R8, RxN; 20 N–N5, R–K2; 21 P–Q6. Instead, he chooses a prettier but more involved line.

(*See Diagram on page 196*)

Position after 18 . . . R–K2

19	N–N5!?	RxN
20	P–KN4!!	Q–R3

There was no good defense, for example 20 . . . Q–N3 (if 20 . . . Q–B2; 21 N–Q6ch wins Black's Queen); 21 Q–R8!, R–K2; 22 P–Q6, R–B2; 23 PxP wins.

If 20 . . . Q–K1; 21 RxPch!, K–Q1; 22 RxQNP, N–Q2; 23 N–Q6!, R–K8ch; 24 K–N2 wins.

If 20 . . . Q–R6; 21 N–Q6ch, K–Q1; 22 N–B7ch wins.

21	RxPch	K–Q1
22	Q–R8	Resigns

Now we can appreciate the fact that the interpolation of White's twentieth move staved off the possibility of . . . R–K8 mate at this point. Bernstein had a razor-sharp style.

KING'S GAMBIT REVISITED

All his life long, Rudolf Spielmann looked back nostalgically to the brilliant gambit chess of his grandfather's day. From time to time he struck quite a few sparks off the ancient anvil.

ALLGAIER GAMBIT

Munich, 1903

	WHITE (R. *Spielmann*)	BLACK (M. *Elyashov*)
1	P–K4	P–K4
2	P–KB4	PxP
3	N–KB3	P–KN4
4	P–KR4	P–N5
5	N–N5!?	. . . .

The modern player may raise his eyebrows at this cavalier sacrifice of a piece, but in the good old days they thought nothing of such a giveaway on the chance of checking once or twice and indulging in some general hell-raising.

5	. . . .	P–KR3
6	NxP	KxN
7	B–B4ch	P–Q4
8	BxPch	K–N2
9	P–Q4	Q–B3?

Too risky. Instead, 9 . . . N–KB3 is a sound developing move.

10	P–K5	Q–KN3
11	P–R5	Q–B4
12	N–B3	B–N5
13	Castles	P–B6
14	N–K4	QxRP
15	N–N3	Q–R5

White has gained considerable time by harrying the Black Queen. Yet the following sacrifice is startling.

(*See Diagram on page 198*)

16	RxP!!	PxR
17	QxP	N–KB3

If 17 . . . Q–K2??; 18 N–R5ch leads to mate.

18	PxNch	K–B1

If 18 . . . K–N3; 19 Q–Q3ch, KxP; 20 B–KB4! wins.

BLACK

WHITE

Position after 15 . . . Q–R5

19	B–KB4!	N–R3

If 19 . . . QxP?; 20 B–Q6ch, K–N2; 21 N–R5ch winning.

Or 19 . . . B–Q3; 20 BxBch, PxB; 21 Q–K3, R–R2; 22 R–K1, B–Q2; 23 BxP and White wins.

20	Q–K4!	Q–N5
21	BxNP!	BxB

On 21 . . . QR–N1; 22 BxN! is decisive (22 . . . BxB; 23 BxPch). But now White wins Black's Queen.

22	BxPch	RxB
23	QxQ	R–R2
24	Q–N6	R–B2
25	P–B3	B–Q3
26	N–B5	B–K5
27	Q–R6ch	K–N1
28	Q–N5ch	K–B1

Or 28 . . . K–R2; 29 Q–R4ch winning easily.

29	N–R6	Resigns

Black is helpless against the coming Q–N8ch. A fine example of relentless attack.

THE TEMPEST

When one of Marshall's impetuous attacks was in full blast, the opposing King was exposed to a raging storm that beat down all opposition.

QUEEN'S GAMBIT DECLINED

Nuremberg, 1906

WHITE (*F. J. Marshall*) BLACK (*E. Cohn*)

1	P–Q4	P–Q4
2	P–QB4	P–K3
3	N–QB3	P–QB4
4	BPxP	KPxP
5	N–B3	N–KB3

A costly inaccuracy on which Marshall immediately pounces. The alternative 5 . . . N–QB3 is much safer.

6	B–N5!	B–K3
7	P–K4!	BPxP
8	B–N5ch!	QN–Q2
9	KNxP	. . . .

Black is already reeling from White's hammer blows. If now 9 . . . PxP; 10 NxB, PxN; 11 BxN, PxB; 12 Q–R5ch with a winning attack for White.

9	. . . .	B–QN5
10	P–K5!	P–KR3
11	PxN	BxNch
12	PxB	PxB
13	NxB	PxN
14	PxP	KR–N1

Black's King-side has been irretrievably smashed up.

15	Q–R5ch	K–K2
16	QxPch	K–B2
17	Q–R5ch	. . . .

In the event of 17 . . . KxP, White will continue 18 R–Q1! followed by R–Q3–N3ch etc.

17	. . . .	K–K2
18	Castles/K	RxP

19	KR–K1	N–B3
20	Q–R3	Q–Q3

One gets a deceptive impression hereabouts that Black is consolidating his game.

21	B–Q3!	QR–KN1
22	P–N3	N–N5
23	B–B5!	N–K4

Now comes the second wave of Marshall's attack.

BLACK

WHITE

Position after 23 . . . N–K4

| 24 | BxP! | R–KB1 |

What else? If 24 . . . QxB; 25 QxQch and 26 P–KB4 and White's win is child's play.

Or 24 . . . N–B6ch; 25 K–R1, NxR; 26 RxN or 26 BxR winning nicely.

25	Q–R4ch	R–B3
26	BxP!	QxB
27	Q–Q4!	K–K3
28	QR–Q1!	Resigns

For after 28 . . . QxQ; 29 PxQ White wins easily, while if 28 . . . R–Q2; 29 RxNch!, QxR; 30 QxR mate. Tarrasch's considered verdict: "A magnificent game."

THE LIFEBLOOD OF CHESS

After we have paid our dutiful respects to such frigid virtues as calculation, foresight, self-control and the like, we always come back to the thought that speculative attack is the lifeblood of chess. In this game, at any rate, White's Pawn sacrifice "on spec" yields rich dividends.

GIUOCO PIANO

Paris, 1909

WHITE (*F. Lazard*) BLACK (*M. Gibaud*)

1	P–K4	P–K4
2	N–KB3	N–QB3
3	B–B4	B–B4
4	P–Q4	PxP
5	P–B3	N–B3

Here 5 . . . PxP; 6 NxP turns the opening into a Scotch Gambit.

6	PxP	B–N5ch
7	N–B3	NxKP
8	Castles	BxN
9	P–Q5	. . . .

The adventurous Moeller Attack, which has the prime purpose of creating confusion in the enemy's ranks.

9	. . . .	B–B3
10	R–K1	N–K2
11	RxN	P–Q3
12	P–KN4	. . . .

This has been given the apt name of the "Bayonet Attack."

12	. . . .	P–KR3

Black is better off with 12 . . . Castles!; 13 P–N5, B–K4 returning the Pawn and leaving White with a somewhat compromised Pawn position.

13	P–KR4	K–B1
14	P–R5!	. . . .

Ruling out . . . N–N3.

14	. . . .	P–KN4

To make room for . . . K–N2.

15	N–Q4	P–B3

16	Q–B3!	NxP
17	B–Q2!	N–B2
18	QR–K1!	P–Q4

Black expects to win a piece, but he has failed to reckon with White's powerful attacking position.

| | 19 | B–N4ch! | K–N2 |

Now comes a whole series of extraordinary moves.

BLACK

WHITE

Position after 19 . . . K–N2

| | 20 | R–K7!! | PxB |

Or 20 . . . BxR; 21 RxB, R–B1; 22 B–B3!!, QxR (if 22 . . . K–N1; 23 Q–B6 wins); 23 N–B5 dbl ch, K–R2; 24 NxQ, PxB; 25 Q–B6, N–K1; 26 Q–N6ch!! and White forces mate.

| | 21 | NxP!! | Q–Q6 |

If 21 . . . PxN; 22 QxBch!! and mate follows.

	22	RxPch!!	KxR
	23	R–K7ch!	K–N1
	24	QxB	R–R2
	25	R–K8ch!	Resigns

If 25 . . . NxR; 26 Q–B8 mate. This glorious game received a well-earned First Brilliancy Prize.

PROVOKING PAWN WEAKNESSES

There is real artistry in the skillful manner that White provokes Pawn weaknesses in Black's castled position. The final fireworks, while equally artistic, are nevertheless easier to understand and to enjoy.

CARO-KANN DEFENSE

Munich, 1909

WHITE (*S. Tartakover*)   BLACK (*H. Fahrni*)

1	P–K4	P–QB3
2	P–Q4	P–Q4
3	N–QB3	PxP
4	NxP	N–B3
5	NxNch	KPxN
6	B–QB4	B–Q3
7	N–K2	Castles

While Black has a free development, his doubled Pawn gives him an unwieldy Pawn position that may lead to difficulties later on.

8	Castles	B–KN5
9	P–KR3	BxN

The simplest solution, but White's Bishops will gain steadily in power from now on.

10	QxB	R–K1
11	Q–R5	. . . .

By taking this aggressive post, White creates a troublesome situation for Black. For example, 11 . . . P–KN3 will not do because of 12 BxPch!, KxB; 13 QxRPch etc.

11	. . . .	Q–K2
12	B–Q2	. . . .

With the venomous threat of 13 QR–K1, Q–B1; 14 QxBPch!, QxQ; 15 RxRch and wins.

12	. . . .	N–Q2
13	KR–K1	Q–B1
14	Q–KB5!	RxRch

Not 14 . . . N–N3; 15 B–Q3 forcing the win of a Pawn as Black must play 15 . . . P–N3.

15	RxR	R–Q1
16	B–Q3!	P–KN3
17	Q–N4	P–KR4

The White Queen was too strongly placed, but meanwhile more weaknesses are created.

	18	Q–K4	B–B2
	19	B–QB4	....

See the previous comment. White threatens 20 QxNPch.

	19	....	K–N2
	20	Q–K3!	....

Renewing the threat, which is now 21 Q–R6ch, K–N1; 22 QxNPch etc.

	20	....	P–KN4
	21	Q–K2	N–N3
	22	B–N3	RxP

Black is desperate. He realizes that after 22 . . . P–R5, White completes the demolition work with 23 P–KB4!

	23	B–B3	Q–Q3

Black threatens mate! White's reply defends—and attacks, too.

BLACK

WHITE

Position after 23 . . . Q–Q3

	24	QxP!	Q–R7ch
	25	K–B1	N–Q4

Now Black hopes for 26 BxR, Q–R8ch; 27 K–K2, N–B5ch; 28 K–Q2, QxRch! etc.

	26	BxN!	RxB
	27	BxPch!	KxB
	28	Q–R6ch	K–B4
	29	P–KN4ch	K–B5

30 Q–B6ch   Resigns

It is mate next move. An exceptionally absorbing game, notable for its masterly blending of strategy and tactics.

THE CHILD IS FATHER OF THE MAN

It is always interesting to examine a World Champion's youthful games to find hints of his later successes. In Alekhine's case this is particularly rewarding, for his tactical exploitation of positional weaknesses was always refreshingly crisp. Here he hammers away energetically at the target presented by Black's enfeebled black squares.

ENGLISH OPENING

Carlsbad, 1911

WHITE (*A. Alekhine*) BLACK (*O. Chajes*)

1	P–QB4	P–K3
2	P–K4	P–QB4
3	N–QB3	N–QB3
4	N–B3	P–KN3?

The combination of Black's first and fourth moves makes a very poor pair because of the serious weakening of his black squares. With 4 . . . N–Q5! he would have had easy equality.

5	P–Q4!	PxP
6	NxP	B–N2
7	N/Q4–N5!	B–K4

Clumsy but necessary. See the previous comment.

8	P–B4	P–QR3

The alternative 8 . . . B–N2; 9 Q–Q6!!—or 8 . . . B–N1; 9 P–K5—is positionally hopeless for Black.

9	PxB	PxN
10	B–B4	PxP
11	BxP	R–R4

Menacing White's King Pawn and also preventing the threatened 12 N–N5 because of 12 . . . RxN! 13 BxR, Q–R4ch and 14 . . . QxB.

12	Castles!	P–QN4

Rightly realizing that his plight would be hopeless after 12 . . .

NxP; 13 BxN, RxB; 14 Q–Q6! etc., Black seeks complications: 13 NxP?, RxN; 14 BxR, Q–N3ch and 15 . . . QxB. But Alekhine outwits him.

	13	P–QN4!	Q–N3ch
	14	K–R1	NxNP
	15	BxNP!	RxB
	16	NxR	QxN

Has White blundered?

BLACK

WHITE

Position after 16 . . . QxN

	17	QR–N1!	. . . .

The point: Black's advanced Knight is lost.

For example: 17 . . . Q–R4; 18 B–Q2. Or 17 . . . Q–B4; 18 R–B1 and wins.

	17	. . . .	B–R3

Threatens . . . QxRch.

	18	Q–Q6!	P–B3

He sees that 18 . . . N–K2 will not do: 19 QxN/N4!, QxQ; 20 RxQ, BxR; 21 R–N8ch and wins.

	19	KR–B1!	Q–Q6

Black is bankrupt.

	20	RxN	P–N4
	21	R–Q4	Q–N4
	22	P–QR4	Q–N2
	23	R–B7	Q–N8ch
	24	R–Q1	Resigns

A delightful bit of fluff.

THE OLD AND THE NEW

What a spectacle! Rudolf Spielmann, self-appointed missionary of the classical King's Gambit, encounters his fellow Viennese Richard Réti, who a few years later is to become one of the founders of the revolutionary school of Hypermodern chess. Spielmann, a veteran at 30, gives his younger opponent a convincing thrashing.

KING'S KNIGHT'S GAMBIT

Abbazia, 1912

	WHITE (R. *Spielmann*)	BLACK (R. *Réti*)
1	P–K4	P–K4
2	P–KB4	PxP
3	N–KB3	N–KB3
4	N–B3	P–Q4
5	P–K5	N–K5
6	B–K2	N–QB3

Black has good chances of seizing the initiative with 6 . . . B–QB4!; 7 P–Q4, B–QN5 etc.

7	P–Q3	NxN
8	PxN	P–KN4
9	Castles	KR–N1
10	P–Q4	P–N5?!

This impetuous rush merely results in an open King Bishop file for White. 10 . . . B–K3 was a reasonable developing move.

11	N–K1	P–B6
12	B–Q3!	Q–R5
13	B–KB4	PxP
14	NxP	Q–R4
15	R–N1!	N–Q1
16	P–B4!	B–K3
17	N–K3!	. . . .

Exploiting the absence of Black's Queen, White presses ahead vehemently in the center.

17	. . . .	PxP
18	B–K4!!	P–QB3
19	P–Q5!	. . . .

This powerful thrust explains White's previous move.

19	. . . .	B–QB4!?

Black realizes that 19 . . . PxP; 20 NxQP, BxN; 21 QxB is hopeless for him.

BLACK

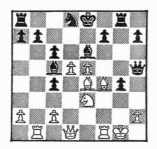

WHITE

Position after 19 . . . B–QB4!?

            20   K–R1!   . . . .
White spurns 20 PxB, NxP; 21 Q–K2, NxB; 22 RxN, QxP which
gives Black four Pawns for the piece.
            20   . . . .   BxN
            21   PxB!   NxP
Not 21 . . . BxB; 22 Q–Q7ch, K–B1; 23 RxB winning.
            22   BxB   QxP
            23   BxRP   R–R1
If 23 . . . R–N2; 24 B–B4!! holds everything.
            24   RxBP!!   R–Q1
And not 24 . . . KxR; 25 Q–Q7ch and 26 R–KB1ch when White
wins.
            25   QxP!   QxB
On 25 . . . KxR; 26 RxPch is decisive.
            26   B–N6!   Resigns
Black's Queen has no refuge from the White Rook's prospective
discovered check. White also threatens 27 R–R7 dis ch etc.

THE OLD MAESTRO

Marshall was the virtuoso of imaginative attacking play. He was always preoccupied with the problem of making chess positions conform to purely imaginary patterns—which is one way to describe what happens in the course of a combination.

PETROFF'S DEFENSE

Match, 1912

	WHITE (*D. Janowski*)	BLACK (*F. J. Marshall*)
1	P–K4	P–K4
2	N–KB3	N–KB3
3	NxP	P–Q3
4	N–KB3	NxP
5	P–Q4	P–Q4
6	B–Q3	B–Q3
7	P–B4?	. . . .

Instead of this premature move, White should castle.

| 7 | . . . . | B–QN5ch |
| 8 | K–B1 | . . . . |

Perhaps too despairing, though it must be admitted that Black retains a fine initiative after 8 QN–Q2, Castles; 9 Castles, BxN; 10 BxB, B–N5 etc.

8	. . . .	Castles
9	PxP	QxP
10	Q–B2	R–K1
11	N–B3	. . . .

Also after 11 BxN, RxB; 12 N–B3, Q–B5ch Black has an excellent game. But who could dream that the plausible-looking text move paves the way for the sacrifice of Black's Queen?

| 11 | . . . . | NxN |
| 12 | PxN | . . . . |

(*See Diagram on page 210*)

| 12 | . . . . | QxN!! |

For if 13 PxQ, B–KR6ch; 14 K–N1, R–K8ch and mate next move.

| 13 | PxB | N–B3 |
| 14 | B–N2 | . . . . |

What else? If 14 B–K3, B–R6!; 15 KR–N1, RxB! wins for Black.

| 14 | . . . . | NxNP! |

BLACK

WHITE

Position after 12 PxN

Although White has guarded against the mate, Marshall continues to leave his Queen *en prise*.

   15 BxPch   K–R1
   16 PxQ   . . . .

The alternative is 16 Q–Q2, B–R6; 17 KR–N1, KxB; 18 PxB, QxRPch; 19 R–N2, Q–Q6ch; 20 QxQ, NxQ with an easy end-game win for Black.

   16 . . . .   B–R6ch
   17 K–N1   NxQ
   18 BxN   R–K7

This is the kind of position that Marshall loved—one attacking move after another!

   19 R–QB1   QR–K1

The point of Black's magnificent combination: he threatens 20 . . . RxB as well as 20 . . . R–K8ch.

   20 B–B3   R/K1–K6!?

Very pretty, though the simpler 20 . . . RxB!; 21 RxR, R–K3 would also serve.

   21 B–N4   . . . .

Here 21 PxR is out of the question; there follows 21 . . . R–N7ch; 22 K–B1, RxB dis ch and then 23 . . . RxRch.

   21 . . . .   R/K6xP
   22 B–Q1   R–B3!!
     Resigns

White has no defense against the threat of . . . R–KN3 mate, for example 23 B–B2, RxB! Glorious tactics!

MODERN GAMBITS

Though we often hear grumbles about the coming death of chess through "over-perfection" of technique, master chess continues to rejuvenate itself. The introduction of early Pawn sacrifices "on spec" is a favored device to this end.

FRENCH DEFENSE

Mannheim, 1914

WHITE *(A. Alekhine)*   BLACK *(H. Fahrni)*

1	P–K4	P–K3
2	P–Q4	P–Q4
3	N–QB3	N–KB3
4	B–N5	B–K2
5	P–K5	KN–Q2
6	P–KR4!	. . . .

This gambit move was first introduced by Alekhine in the present game. Nowadays Black never accepts the Pawn offer.

6	. . . .	BxB
7	PxB	QxP?

Too time-consuming. White gains ample time to build up a powerful position.

8	N–R3	Q–K2
9	N–B4	N–B1
10	Q–N4!	. . . .

White threatens 11 NxQP! in addition to 11 QxNP.

10	. . . .	P–KB4
11	PxP *e.p.*	PxP
12	Castles	. . . .

This renews the threat of NxQP.

12	. . . .	P–B3
13	R–K1	K–Q1
14	R–R6!	P–K4

White's pieces have developed a menacing attack, and the text only helps him.

15	Q–R4	QN–Q2
16	B–Q3	P–K5

(See Diagram on page 212)

BLACK

WHITE

Position after 16 . . . P–K5

17 Q–N3!   . . . .

The blocked position is deceptive. White has renewed the threat of NxQP!

17 . . . .   Q–B2

Or 17 . . . Q–Q3; 18 BxP!, PxB; 19 RxKP! and wins.

18 BxP!   PxB

19 NxP   KR–N1

A curious possibility here is 19 . . . QxP; 20 NxP!, NxN; 21 Q–N7 and White wins.

20 Q–QR3!   Q–N2

Or 20 . . . Q–K2; 21 Q–R5ch, P–N3; 22 Q–B3 and Black is helpless.

21 N–Q6   N–QN3

If 21 . . . QxR; 22 N–B7ch wins Black's Queen.

22 N–K8   Q–KB2

If 22 . . . Q–Q2; 23 NxP wins—or 22 . . . N–B5; 23 Q–B5, Q–B2; 24 RxBP and again White triumphs.

23 Q–Q6ch   Resigns

It is mate in two. A strikingly original game by White.

HYPERMODERN CHESS

After World War I there sprang up a school of chess thought that mirrored the postwar world of inflation, putsches, and famine. The outstanding Hypermodern theorist was Julius Breyer, who died at a very young age. His close friend Richard Réti described him as "that man, so sagacious that the finest finesses were not fine enough for him, and who at a glance saw through the most complicated conditions . . ." And Réti added that Breyer "had moreover at his command an untiring and intellectual capacity for work." It is rather anticlimactic to find this genius daunted by simple common sense in the following game.

QUEEN'S GAMBIT DECLINED

Budapest, 1919

WHITE (*J. Breyer*)   BLACK (*R. Réti*)

	WHITE	BLACK
1	P–Q4	P–Q4
2	P–K3	N–KB3
3	N–Q2	. . . .

This slow and cramped development was typical of Breyer's original style.

	WHITE	BLACK
3	. . . .	B–B4
4	P–QB4	P–B3
5	PxP	PxP
6	B–N5ch!?	. . . .

Black is to be tempted to play . . . P–QR3 and . . . P–QN4 later on, weakening his black squares.

	WHITE	BLACK
6	. . . .	QN–Q2
7	KN–B3	P–QR3
8	B–R4	P–K3
9	Q–K2	. . . .

Making room for his King Bishop at Queen 1!

	WHITE	BLACK
9	. . . .	P–R3

To have a retreat in the event of White's N–R4.

	WHITE	BLACK
10	N–K5	P–QN4
11	NxN	NxN
12	B–Q1!	B–Q3
13	Castles	Castles
14	N–N3	Q–B2
15	P–B4	. . . .

Having seemingly established his mastery of the black squares, Breyer now intends B–Q2–R5.

BLACK ·

WHITE

Position after 15 P–B4

| 15 . . . . | P–QR4!? |

This ingenious Pawn sacrifice is all the more enterprising as 15 . . . KR–N1; 16 B–Q2, P–QR4 would have left Black with an excellent game.

| 16 QxP | P–R5 |

Black has the initiative.

17	N–Q2	KR–N1
18	Q–K2	N–B3
19	N–B3	N–K5
20	N–R4	N–B6!

It takes six more moves to establish the point of this clever sacrifice. Even if White declines it Black still obtains a decisive grip on the position with . . . NxB.

21	PxN	QxP
22	NxB	PxN
23	B–B2	QxR
24	B–R3?!	QxRP
25	BxB	R–N7
26	R–B1	P–R6!
	Resigns	

There is nothing to be done against Black's threat of 27 . . . RxB!; 28 RxR, QxR!; 29 QxQ, P–R7 etc. Réti has proved himself the better tactician.

THE ORTHODOXY OF ECCENTRICITY

In the following game we see Breyer's sharply original style at its very best. Almost every move he makes comes as a surprise. Such games created a vogue for unconventional play that took a decade to run its course.

NIMZOVICH DEFENSE

Vienna, 1920

WHITE (*M. Euwe*) BLACK (*J. Breyer*)

1	P–K4	N–QB3
2	N–QB3	N–B3
3	P–Q4	P–K4
4	PxP	QNxP
5	P–B4	N–B3
6	P–K5	N–KN1

Black does not mind retreating, as he is convinced that White's King Pawn is weak.

7	B–B4	. . . .

The alternative 7 N–B3, P–Q3; 8 B–N5! is more likely to give White a strong grip on the position.

7	. . . .	P–Q3
8	N–B3	B–N5
9	Castles	Q–Q2
10	Q–K1!?	Castles!
11	N–KN5	PxP!

Black sees that a quiet course will not do: 11 . . . N–R3; 12 NxBP!, NxN; 13 P–K6! etc.

12	K–R1	. . . .

White's omission of 12 NxBP is puzzling at first sight, but after 12 . . . Q–Q5ch; 13 K–R1, QxB; 14 NxKR his venturesome Knight would be trapped.

12	. . . .	P–B3!
13	N–B7	N–R4!
14	NxQR	NxB
15	Q–K4	N–Q3
16	Q–N4	. . . .

Apparently very strong because of the threat of 17 NxP! And on 16 . . . KxN or 16 . . . QxN or . . . N–R3, White has an advantageous reply in 17 PxP!

BLACK

WHITE

Position after 16 Q–N4

16 . . . .   B–K2!!

With this move Black wins the fantastic duel of wits. But White still has some fight left in him.

17	PxP	PxP
18	NxP	NxN
19	R–B8ch!?	BxR
20	QxBch	Q–Q1!

Black has made his point by winning the Knight, but he must still play with care. For example, after 20 . . . N–Q1 the continuation 21 B–N5, P–KR3; 22 BxN, QxB; 23 QxP etc. is still troublesome.

21	QxP	N–B3
22	B–N5	R–N1!

For if 23 QxN, RxB wins.

23	Q–R6	R–N3
24	Q–R4	N–Q3
25	R–KB1	N–B4
26	QxB	NxQ
27	BxQ	N/N5–K6!

The rest is silence.

28	R–B3	KxB
29	P–KR3	R–N6
30	RxR	NxRch
	Resigns	

One of the best games of a legendary genius.

ONE-TRACK MIND

The German master Carl Carls—even his name suggests uniformity—always started his games with the White pieces with 1 P–QB4. He turned it into a fearsome weapon, but every now and then he came a cropper. This was one of the occasions.

ENGLISH OPENING

Gothenburg, 1920

WHITE	(C. Carls)	BLACK	(M. Euwe)
1	P–QB4	P–K3	
2	N–QB3	P–QB4	
3	P–K4	N–QB3	
4	P–B4	KN–K2!	

Black is angling for . . . P–Q4, after which he will fianchetto his King Bishop for lasting pressure along the long diagonal, specifically against White's Queen 4 square, which is a hole.

5	N–B3	P–Q4	
6	P–Q3	P–KN3!	
7	B–K2	B–N2	
8	Castles	Castles	
9	B–Q2	N–Q5	
10	B–K1	P–N3	
11	B–R4	B–N2	

Black has the better game because of his grip on the Queen 5 square. In addition, both of his Bishops have ample scope.

| 12 | BPxP | PxP | |

Black does not fear 13 PxP, for then 12 . . . N/Q5–B4! will recover the Pawn advantageously.

13	NxN	BxNch	
14	K–R1	Q–Q2	
15	P–B5	. . . .	

White wants to attack at all cost. Black has an elegant refutation.

15	. . . .	QPxP	
16	QPxP	PxP	
17	PxP	NxP!	

For if 18 B–N4, NxB!; 19 BxQ, BxP mate.

18	B–B2	K–R1!
19	B–N4	. . . .

Apparently killing, but Black has a fine reply.

BLACK

WHITE

Position after 19 B–N4

19	. . . .	R–KN1!
20	BxBch	PxB

And now in the event of 21 BxN, Black wins with 21 . . . BxPch; 22 K–N1, BxR dis ch; 23 KxB, QxBch etc.

21	RxN	RxB!
22	QxR	R–KN1
23	QxRch	. . . .

On 23 R–KN5, QxQ wins easily for Black. Or if 23 Q–B4, BxPch; 24 K–N1, B–K5 dis ch, again with an easy win for Black.

23	. . . .	KxQ
24	R–KN5ch	K–B1
25	N–Q1	. . . .

White is lost. If 25 N–K2 (or 25 R–Q1), Q–K2 wins a piece. Or if 25 N–N5, P–KR3; 26 R–K5 (or 26 R–KR5, Q–N5), P–B3; 27 R–KB1, K–N2 and Black still wins a piece.

25	. . . .	Q–K2

Resigns

For after 26 P–KR4, Black wins a Rook with 26 . . . Q–K8ch; 27 K–R2, QxPch etc. A charming game.

SURPRISE!

The aspect of Alekhine's combinative play that impressed many observers over the years was that his tactical surprises generally came at the end of a combination rather than at the beginning. Here, for example, he transforms a routine exchanging maneuver into a blazing combination.

QUEEN'S INDIAN DEFENSE

Triberg, 1921

WHITE (*A. Alekhine*)   BLACK (*E. Bogolyubov*)

	WHITE	BLACK
1	P–Q4	N–KB3
2	N–KB3	P–K3
3	P–B4	P–QN3
4	P–KN3	B–N2
5	B–N2	P–B4

After this questionable move Black is bound to run into difficulties on the long diagonal. The alternative 5 . . . B–K2 is preferable.

| 6 | PxP | . . . . |

An even stronger line is 6 P–Q5!, PxP; 7 N–R4 whereby White recovers the Pawn advantageously and seriously cramps Black's position.

6	. . . .	BxP
7	Castles	Castles
8	N–B3	P–Q4

Black naturally wants to rid himself of his backward Queen Pawn. But this enables White to set up an annoying pin, which in turn induces Black to part with one of his Bishops. The upshot is that White's Queen takes up an aggressive position.

9	N–Q4!	BxN
10	QxB	N–B3
11	Q–R4	PxP
12	R–Q1!	Q–B1

This rules out the participation of Black's Queen in the defense, but after 12 . . . Q–K2; 13 B–N5! is very strong.

| 13 | B–N5! | N–Q4 |

As 13 . . . N–Q2; 14 N–K4 leaves White with a powerful attack, White plausibly seeks relief in simplifying exchanges.

| 14 | NxN | PxN |
| 15 | RxP! | N–N5 |

BLACK

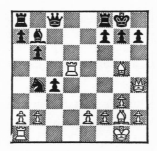

WHITE

Position after 15 . . . N–N5

16 B–K4!!   . . . .

The sudden mate threat comes as a stunning surprise. If Black plays
16 . . . P–N3 there follows 17 B–B6!, NxR; 18 BxN, P–KR4 (if 18
. . . BxB; 19 Q–R6 is fatal for Black); 19 B–QB3!! and 20
Q–B6 is the winning threat.

The alternative is 16 . . . P–KR3; 17 BxP, P–B4; 18 Q–N5, Q–B2;
19 BxNP!, QxB; 20 QxQch, KxQ; 21 R–Q7ch and White wins easily.

16	. . . .	P–B4
17	BxP!	RxB
18	R–Q8ch	. . . .

This is really the point of White's combination. He wins the Black
Queen, and the rest more or less plays itself.

18	. . . .	QxR
19	BxQ	QR–B1
20	R–Q1	R–KB2
21	Q–N4	N–Q6
22	PxN	RxB
23	PxP	QR–KB1
24	P–B4	R–K2
25	K–B2	P–KR3
26	R–K1	B–B1
27	Q–B3	R/K2–KB2
28	Q–Q5	P–KN4
29	R–K7	PxP
30	PxP	Resigns

White is bound to win on simple material advantage. White's charming combination was rewarded with a First Brilliancy Prize.

CROSSING IN MIDSTREAM

White starts off too conservatively and then switches to a daring policy—castling Queen-side. As his position is not geared for aggressive tactics, his King becomes the target of an attack pursued by Rubinstein with his usual skill.

QUEEN'S PAWN OPENING

London, 1922

WHITE (*V. Wahltuch*)   BLACK (*A. Rubinstein*)

1	P–Q4	N–KB3
2	N–KB3	P–K3
3	B–N5	P–B4
4	BxN	QxB
5	P–K3	. . . .

White's opening lacks bite.

5	. . . .	N–B3
6	P–B3	B–K2
7	B–Q3	P–Q4
8	QN–Q2	Castles
9	Q–K2	. . . .

Slow. With 9 PxP, BxP; 10 P–K4, White could still obtain a presentable position. Now Black seizes the initiative.

9	. . . .	P–K4!
10	PxKP	NxP
11	NxN	QxN
12	Castles/Q?	. . . .

Castling on the other wing was much safer, though Black's freer game and two Bishops would give him decidedly better prospects.

12	. . . .	P–QN4!

This enterprising Pawn offer tempts White to capture and thus open the Queen Knight file for Black's Rooks.

13	N–B3	Q–B2
14	BxP?	R–N1
15	B–Q3	Q–R4

BLACK

WHITE

Position after 15 . . . Q–R4

Defending the Queen Rook Pawn is not so easy for White, for example 16 P–QR3, P–B5; 17 B–N1, RxP!!; 18 KxR (if 18 QxR, BxP wins White's Queen), B–KB4!! (threatens 19 . . . QxRP mate); 19 BxB, QxRPch; 20 K–B2, Q–R7ch; 21 K–B1, B–R6ch and mate next move.

| 16 B–N1 | B–B3 |
| 17 R–Q2? | . . . . |

A weak move in a critical situation. 17 Q–Q2 was his best chance.

| 17 . . . . | B–R3! |

With this pretty idea in mind: 18 B–Q3, QxP!; 19 BxB, Q–R8ch; 20 K–B2, RxPch; 21 K–Q3, QxBch and mate follows.

| 18 Q–Q1 | BxP! |

For 19 PxB allows Black a mate in two.

| 19 BxPch | K–R1! |

Stronger than 19 . . . KxB; 20 Q–B2ch followed by 21 QxB.

| 20 Q–B2 | RxP |
| 21 RxP?! | QxP! |

Even stronger than capturing White's Queen.

| 22 R–R5 | . . . . |

A sly trap: if 22 . . . RxQch; 23 BxR dis ch and White has a perpetual check!

22	Q–R8ch!
23 Q–N1	RxQch
Resigns	

Note the finesse of Black's play: after 24 BxR dis ch, K–N1 White has no perpetual check, as his Bishop is pinned. On the surface there is nothing remarkable about this game; the fireworks are all in the variations that never happened.

NOW OR NEVER

The textbooks tell us to castle early in order to get the King in a safe position. To castle early, we need to get the King-side pieces developed fairly quickly. All this is so obvious that we accept it unthinkingly. We are therefore apt to be brought up with a jolt when we see the gruesome consequences of neglected castling.

QUEEN'S GAMBIT DECLINED

Dutch Championship, 1924

	WHITE (*M. Euwe*)	BLACK (*A. Speyer*)
1	P–Q4	P–Q4
2	N–KB3	N–KB3
3	P–K3	P–B3
4	P–B4	P–K3
5	QN–Q2	P–B4

The loss of time in moving this Pawn twice should not be serious if Black plays accurately from now on. For example, his next move should be . . . N–B3 with strong pressure on the center.

6	B–Q3	QN–Q2
7	Castles	P–QN3?

Fianchettoing his Queen Bishop is a good idea, but most untimely here. Correct was 7 . . . B–K2 and 8 . . . Castles.

8	BPxP!	KPxP
9	P–K4!	B–N2
10	KPxP!	BxP
11	R–K1ch	. . . .

With a few energetic strokes White has opened up the position and gives Black no rest from this point on.

11	. . . .	B–K2
12	PxP	NxP
13	B–N5ch	K–B1

Black pays the penalty for his dawdling. The reasonable-looking 13 . . . QN–Q2 is answered by 14 Q–K2, preventing Black from castling.

14	P–QN3	B–N2
15	B–N2	N–Q6
16	B/N5xN!	. . . .

Stronger than 16 B/N2xN, BxB!; 17 R–K8ch, QxR; 18 BxQ, BxR etc.

16	. . . .	QxB
17	QR–B1	R–Q1

BLACK

WHITE

Position after 17 . . . R–Q1

18 RxB!! . . . .

This sacrifice of the Exchange has some glittering points. To begin with: if 18 . . . KxR; 19 B–R3ch, K–K1; 20 Q–K1ch, N–K5; 21 R–B7!, R–Q2; 22 RxB!, RxR; 23 NxN and White wins.

18 . . . . BxN

19 B–R3!! . . . .

Black cannot very well answer this spectacular move with 19 . . . BxQ, for then 20 R–K3 dis ch leaves White a clear piece ahead (20 . . . K–N1; 21 RxQ, RxR??; 22 R–B8ch forcing mate).

And on 19 . . . K–N1; 20 PxB! leaves White with a winning advantage.

19 . . . . Q–R3

Now White's game seems in a very precarious state.

20 R/B1–B7! QxB

But not 20 . . . BxQ; 21 RxBP dbl ch and White mates next move.

      21   RxBPch   K–K1

After 21 . . . K–N1; 22 RxNPch leads to much the same conclusion.

      22   Q–K1ch   Resigns

The finish might have been 22 . . . N–K5; 23 NxN, R–Q8; 24 N–Q6 dbl ch and mate next move. Such dashing attacks are unusual in the "close" openings.

STRONG OR WEAK?

In the exciting Four Pawns' Variation of this opening the balance is poised very delicately between White's attacking chances and Black's pressure on the White Pawns. One inexactitude is enough to decide the fate of the game.

ALEKHINE'S DEFENSE

Hague, 1928

WHITE (*O. Naegeli*) BLACK (*A. Muffang*)

1	P–K4	N–KB3
2	P–K5	N–Q4
3	P–QB4	N–N3
4	P–Q4	P–Q3
5	P–B4	PxP
6	BPxP	. . . .

Black's provocative first move has evoked an aggressive reaction from White.

6	. . . .	N–B3
7	B–K3	B–B4
8	N–QB3	P–K3
9	B–K2	B–K2
10	N–B3	P–B3

Black "puts the question" to White's Pawn center.

11	Castles	Castles
12	PxP	BxP
13	Q–Q2	Q–K2
14	QR–Q1	QR–Q1

So far White has played well and he should now reduce the pressure on his center with 15 Q–B1!, B–N5; 16 N–K4!, BxN; 17 NxBch! This continuation would have the incidental virtue of leaving him with two Bishops against two Knights.

15   P–B5?   . . . .

This damages White's Pawn structure irreparably.

15 . . . .   N–Q4

A magnificent square for the Knight.

16   P–QR3   K–R1
17   B–QB4   NxB
18   QxN   B–N5!

Already Black threatens to win the Queen Pawn by . . . BxN etc.

19   N–K2   BxN
20   RxB   . . . .

White is hoping for 20 . . . N–K4; 21 R–R3!, NxB; 22 Q–Q3 when he regains the piece.

BLACK

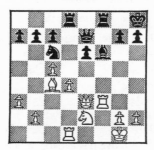

WHITE

Position after 20 RxB

20 . . . .   BxP!!

The first point is that after 21 NxB, RxR; 22 PxR, QxP Black has a pin that regains the piece for him.

21   RxB   NxR
22   NxN   QxP
23   RxRch   RxR

White has two pieces for a Rook, but he must lose a piece no matter how he plays. For example, if he plays 24 P–QN3 there follows 24 . . . P–QN4! and on any move of the Bishop, 25 . . . R–Q1 wins a piece.

On the other hand, if 24 BxKP, R–Q1; 25 N–B5, QxQch; 26 NxQ, R–K1 wins a piece just the same.

24   B–N3   . . . .

Again, if 24 B–R2, R–Q1 wins a piece.

24   . . . .   R–Q1
Resigns

Even now White must lose a piece: 25 N–B2, QxQch; 26 NxQ, R–Q6 etc. The pinning motif reigned supreme.

SUICIDE OR MURDER?

A good case could be made for the argument that Black's handling of the early middle game is suicidal. Yet that would hardly be fair to White, who exploits his opportunities with elegant, pointed attacking moves and thereby admirably earns his victory.

QUEEN'S GAMBIT DECLINED

Rogaska–Slatina, 1929

WHITE (S. Flohr)   BLACK (F. Saemisch)

	WHITE (S. Flohr)	BLACK (F. Saemisch)
1	P–Q4	N–KB3
2	P–QB4	P–K3
3	P–QR3	. . . .

This strange-looking move avoids the Nimzoindian Defense (3 . . . B–N5 in reply to 3 N–QB3).

3	. . . .	P–Q4
4	N–QB3	B–K2
5	B–N5	Castles
6	P–K3	P–QN3
7	PxP	PxP
8	B–Q3	B–N2
9	KN–K2!	. . . .

The Knight heads for the King Bishop 5 square, where it will be powerfully placed.

9	. . . .	QN–Q2
10	N–N3	N–K1

Finding himself in an uncomfortable position, Black seeks a simplifying exchange.

11 P–KR4!   . . . .

A malicious reply with some witty points. For example, on 11 . . . BxB? White wins with 12 BxPch!, KxB; 13 PxB dis ch followed by 14 Q–R5. On 11 . . . P–KB3; 12 Q–R5! leads to decisive sacrifices.

Finally, on 11 . . . P–KR3 White has 12 BxP!, PxB; 13 Q–N4ch, N–N2; 14 N–R5, B–KB3; 15 Q–B4!! and wins (15 . . . NxN; 16 QxRP etc.).

11	. . . .	P–N3
12	B–KR6	N–N2
13	P–R5!	P–KB4

Black allows the opening of the King Rook file as he is understandably repelled by 13 . . . P–KN4; 14 Q–B2 (the simplest, though Q–N4 and N–B5 are also good) when White wins a Pawn.

14	PxP	PxP
15	Q–B3!	P–B3
16	QN–K2	B–Q3
17	Castles/Q	Q–B3
18	R–R3	. . . .

The doubling of White's Rooks on the open file must be decisive.

18 . . . .   K–B2

Here 18 . . . R–B2 was safer.

19 BxN   QxB

BLACK

WHITE

Position after 19 . . . *QxB*

20 BxP!   N–B3

If 20 . . . PxB; 21 NxP, K–N1; 22 NxQ!, RxQ; 23 PxR, KxN; 24 R–N1ch and White wins more material with an easy victory.

21 N–B4   BxN

If 21 . . . PxB; 22 NxBP is absolutely decisive.

22 QxB   QR–K1

Or 22 . . . PxB; 23 NxP, QxP; 24 Q–B7ch forcing the win of Black's Queen.

23 QR–R1   K–N1

If instead 23 . . . PxB; 24 NxP, QxP; 25 N–Q6ch, K–K2; 26 R–R7ch and White wins.

24 R–R8ch!   Resigns

For if 24 . . . K–B2, White has a winning reply in 25 BxPch!; while if 24 . . . QxR; 25 RxQch, KxR; 26 Q–R6ch is decisive. The preservation of White's sacrificial Bishop seems miraculous.

TRUE OR FALSE?

Many chessboard opportunities are not what they seem. They may look attractive at first glance while harboring more somber possibilities that make them ultimately unfavorable.

QUEEN'S GAMBIT DECLINED

Budapest, 1933

WHITE (*J. Szekely*)   BLACK (*E. Canal*)

1	P–Q4	P–Q4
2	P–QB4	P–QB3
3	N–QB3	PxP
4	P–K3	P–QN4
5	NxP?!	. . . .

White sees he can win the Exchange if the Knight is captured. What he forgets is that he will lose valuable time with his Queen.

5	. . . .	PxN!
6	Q–B3	Q–B2
7	QxR	B–N2
8	QxP	P–K3

Black threatens to win the White Queen with . . . N–QB3.

9	P–Q5	PxP
10	Q–Q4	N–KB3
11	N–B3	B–N5ch

12	B–Q2	N–B3
13	BxB!?	. . . .

White hopes for 13 . . . NxQ; 14 NxN with a solid defensive game and more than enough material for his Queen.

BLACK

WHITE

Position after 13 BxB!?

13	. . . .	NxB!

Now Black threatens . . . N–B7ch. If White tries 14 Q–K5ch, QxQ; 15 NxQ, Black has a won game after 15 . . . N–B7ch; 16 K–Q2, NxR; 17 B–K2, N–K5ch; 18 K–B1, P–B3! etc.

14	Q–B3	Q–R4

Black renews the threat of . . . N–B7ch.

15	N–Q2	P–Q5!

This well-timed Pawn sacrifice brings Black's other Knight into powerful play.

16	PxP	KN–Q4
17	Q–KN3	Castles
18	K–Q1	. . . .

After 18 R–B1, Black continues his attack with . . . R–K1ch.

18	. . . .	Q–R5ch
19	P–N3	Q–R6
20	PxP	N–B6ch
21	K–K1	N–B7 mate

Not an unexpected result considering White's losses of time, neglected development, and his useless Queen.

TREAD SOFTLY

In the opening it behooves Black to develop his pieces before embarking on counterplay. If he commits himself too soon he may find himself overwhelmed by superior forces.

QUEEN'S GAMBIT DECLINED

Warsaw, 1935

WHITE (*G. Stahlberg*)   BLACK (*M. Monticelli*)

	WHITE	BLACK
1	P–Q4	N–KB3
2	P–QB4	P–K3
3	N–QB3	P–Q4
4	N–B3	QN–Q2
5	B–N5	P–B3
6	P–K3	Q–R4

The Cambridge Springs Defense, one of Black's better lines in this opening.

7	PxP	NxP
8	Q–Q2	B–N5
9	R–B1	P–QB4

All very enterprising, but Stahlberg reacts aggressively.

10	P–K4	N/Q4–B3
11	B–Q3	PxP
12	NxP	Castles
13	Castles	N–B4?

This definitely leads to trouble. He should have played the more conservative 13 . . . B–K2.

14	BxN!	PxB

Naturally this breakup of Black's King-side Pawns is a very serious matter, but he sees that after 14 . . . NxB he will lose a Pawn: 15 BxP, NxR; 16 BxR, BxN; 17 PxB, KxB; 18 RxN etc.

15	P–QR3!	NxB

After 15 . . . BxN; 16 RxB, NxB; 17 QxN, Black's position remains compromised, for example 17 . . . Q–Q1; 18 Q–N3ch, K–R1; 19 R–Q3, Q–K2; 20 KR–Q1 etc.

16	PxB!!	. . . .

A surprising and original Pawn sacrifice that enables White to gain time for a winning attack.

16 . . . .   NxP/N5
17 QN–N5!   . . . .

Shutting off Black's Queen from the King-side.

BLACK

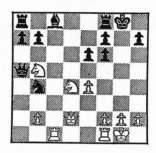

WHITE

Position after 17 QN–N5!

Black realizes that the most obvious reply (17 . . . P–K4) will not do because of 18 R–B3!, PxN; 19 R–KN3ch, K–R1; 20 Q–R6 and White forces mate.

17 . . . .   N–B3
18 R–B3!   R–Q1

Hoping that his King can escape and relying on the double pin for counterplay. In addition, Black threatens 19 . . . QxN.

19 Q–R6!   N–K2

The Knight must be ready to play to Knight 3 after R–KN3ch.

20 QxBP   N–N3

If 20 . . . Q–N5; 21 R–KN3ch is deadly.

21 N–B7!   . . . .

Double attack!

21 . . . .   RxN
22 QxR   Resigns

For if 22 . . . R–N1; 23 Q–Q8ch and Black gets mated after 23 . . . N–B1; 24 R–KN3ch or loses his Queen after 24 . . . K–N2; 25 N–K8ch. Strikingly original attacking play!

THE ISSUE JOINED

In an opening that is supposed to call for judicious position play, White aims for a quick initiative. Black, far from intimidated, hits back smartly. The result is a Donnybrook Fair in which White gets badly mauled.

KING'S INDIAN DEFENSE

Mar del Plata, 1936

WHITE (C. *Guimard*) BLACK (R. *Flores*)

1	P–Q4	N–KB3
2	P–QB4	P–KN3
3	P–KN3	B–N2
4	B–N2	P–Q4
5	PxP	NxP
6	P–K4	. . . .

To White's way of thinking, this Pawn center is formidable. Not so, says Black.

6	. . . .	N–N3
7	N–K2	P–QB4!

Perhaps White will reply 8 PxP, whereupon 8 . . . QxQch; 9 KxQ, N–R5 gives Black much the better game. Or if 8 P–Q5, P–K3! with a good game for Black.

8	P–QR4!?	N–B3!
9	P–Q5	N–Q5
10	P–R5	B–N5!

A surprise and naturally much better than the colorless 10 . . . N–Q2. White's best reply is 11 QN–B3.

11	P–B3?!	NxPch
12	BxN	BxB
13	PxN	BxR
14	K–B2	. . . .

(*See Diagram on page 234*)

14	. . . .	Castles!

Even more enterprising than 14 . . . BxKP; 15 Q–R4ch, K–B1; 16 QxB, QxNP or 14 . . . QxNP; 15 QxB, BxP; 16 BxB, QxB; 17 QN–B3, Q–N3 etc.

15	QxB	P–B4!

BLACK

WHITE

Position after 14 K–B2

16 P–K5   . . . .

White prevents the opening of the King Bishop file—for the time being, anyhow.

16 . . . .   QxNP
17 N–Q2   . . . .

In the event of 17 B–B4, Black has a forceful reply in 17 . . . P–N4.

17 . . . .   P–B5 dis ch!
18 K–B1   BxP
19 NxP   Q–N6!

A tricky reply, for on 20 N–Q2? or 20 NxB, Black wins a piece with 20 . . . Q–Q8ch!

20 N–K3   P–B5!
21 PxP   BxBP
22 NxB   RxNch
23 K–K1   . . . .

If 23 K–N2, QR–KB1; 24 Q–K1, Q–Q6; 25 R–R3, Q–K5ch; 26 K–N1, Q–K4! is decisively in Black's favor.

23 . . . .   R–QB1
24 Q–N2   . . . .

This has all the earmarks of a time-pressure move, but after 24 B–Q2, QxNP; 25 R–Q1, P–QN4 the further advance of Black's Queen-side Pawns should win for him.

24 . . . .   RxBch!
Resigns

For after 25 RxR, QxNch Black wins the Rook as well. Black's vigorous attack has produced a very enjoyable game.

TROJAN HORSES

Games started with Réti's Opening can often unfold with maddeningly portentous slowness. But sometimes, as in this case, the encounter livens up if Black is aggressive-minded. Ultimately a stuning Queen sacrifice allows the decisive infiltration of two Black Knights.

Réti's Opening

Match, 1937

WHITE (A. O'Kelly)	BLACK (P. Devos)
1 N–KB3	N–KB3
2 P–B4	P–B3
3 P–QN3	P–KN3
4 B–N2	B–N2
5 P–N3	Castles
6 B–N2	P–Q4
7 Castles	N–R3

Not a very promising post for this Knight; but it hardly matters, since the players are obviously in a mood for a jog-trot development.

8 P–Q3	B–K3
9 QN–Q2	Q–B1
10 R–K1	. . . .

To prevent the exchange of Bishops by . . . B–R6. But 10 N–N5 serves the same purpose, with the additional virtue of readying 11 P–K4 as a reply to 10 . . . B–B4.

10	B–R6
11 B–R1	P–R4
12 QR–B1	Q–B4
13 P–R3	B–R3!
14 P–QN4	N–N5

While White tries to control the Queen-side by positional means, his opponent, with equal determination, masses his forces for a direct attack on White's King.

15	PxP	PxP
16	P–N5	N–N1
17	R–B5	N–K6!

The first storm warning. If 18 PxN, BxP mate!

18	Q–N3	N–Q2
19	R–B7	P–K4
20	Q–B3	P–Q5
21	NxP?	. . . .

This is one of the most unfortunate things that can happen on a chessboard: White plays a move that despite its clever appearance, is a fearful blunder.

White anticipates 21 . . . PxN?; 22 QxP recovering the piece because of the threatened mate.

BLACK

WHITE

Position after 21 NxP?

21	. . . .	QxPch!!
22	KxQ	N–N5ch
23	K–B3	P–K5ch!
24	KxP	. . . .

Other captures allow 24 . . . N/Q2–K4 mate.

24	. . . .	N/Q2–B3ch
25	K–B3	N–K4ch
26	K–B2	N/B3–N5ch
27	K–N1	B–K6 mate

One of the most elegant mates ever achieved in practical play.

VARIATIONS ON A THEME

Since Emanuel Lasker brought off his beautiful two-Bishop sacrifice against Bauer in the Amsterdam tournament of 1889, variants on this delightful theme have been appearing from time to time. One of the most striking appears in the following game. While the characteristic BxKNP sacrifice is employed here, the remaining Bishop stays to play a dominant role.

QUEEN'S GAMBIT DECLINED

Jurata, 1937

	WHITE (*I. Appel*)	BLACK (*L. Kremer*)
1	P–Q4	P–Q4
2	P–QB4	P–K3
3	N–QB3	P–QB4
4	BPxP	BPxP!?

This Pawn, dignified with the name of the Schara—Hennig Gambit, always leads to interesting attacking play.

5	Q–R4ch	B–Q2
6	QxQP	PxP
7	QxQP	N–QB3
8	P–K3	N–B3
9	Q–N3	B–Q3
10	N–B3	. . . .

The alternative 10 QxP? is much too dangerous because of 10 . . . N–QN5!

10	. . . .	B–K3
11	Q–Q1	. . . .

Likewise after 11 QxP, N–QN5; 12 Q–N5ch, B–Q2; 13 Q–K2, White also gets an uncomfortable game.

11	. . . .	Castles
12	B–K2	Q–K2
13	N–Q4	. . . .

Castling immediately was preferable. White will sorely miss this Knight later on.

13	. . . .	NxN
14	PxN	N–Q4!
15	NxN	BxN

| 16 | Castles | QR–K1! |
| 17 | B–K3 | . . . . |

This leads to trouble, but White has no good moves. For example,
17 B–B3? is met by . . . B–QB5!

| 17 | . . . . | Q–R5! |
| 18 | P–KR3 | . . . . |

He must dismiss 18 P–KN3, which costs a piece after the reply 18
. . . Q–K5!

BLACK

WHITE

Position after 18 P–KR3

| 18 | . . . . | RxB!! |
| 19 | PxR | BxNP! |

For if 20 KxB, Q–N6ch and mate next move.

| 20 | B–B3 | BxP! |

Again threatening mate with 21 . . . Q–N6ch! etc.

21	Q–K2	Q–N6ch
22	K–R1	BxR
23	RxB	R–K1!

Now Black threatens 24 . . . RxP!

24	R–B2	B–B5!
25	P–K4	R–QB1!
26	R–B1	R–B3!
	Resigns	

White is helpless against the coming . . . R–KR3ch. Black's timing
was superb.

MORE VARIATIONS ON A THEME

Even more spectacular than the two-Bishop sacrifice is the two-Rook sacrifice. It takes imagination of the highest order to make such a heavy investment pay off. Yet examples have been known ever since Anderssen's famous 1851 game against Kieseritzky. Here is a notably creative example of the genre.

SICILIAN DEFENSE

Budapest, 1937

WHITE (*S. Boros*)	BLACK (*L. Szabo*)
1 P–K4	P–QB4
2 N–KB2	P–K3
3 P–Q4	PxP
4 NxP	N–KB3
5 N–QB3	P–Q3
6 B–K2	B–K2
7 Castles	Castles

This defensive system, known as the Scheveningen Variation, is losing favor because of its cramped character, which generally exposes Black to a formidable attack.

8 P–B4	P–QR3
9 B–B3	QN–Q2

The more customary . . . N–B3 gives Black a more substantial grip on the center squares.

10 K–R1	Q–B2
11 Q–K1	N–B4
12 P–QN3!	B–Q2
13 B–N2	QR–B1
14 P–K5!	. . . .

This move, driving off Black's valuable protective Knight, officially announces the opening of White's attack.

14	N–K1
15 N–K4!	NxN
16 BxN	P–KN3

Of course, 16 . . . PxP; 17 PxP, QxKP?? would cost Black his Queen after 18 BxPch etc.

17 R–B3!	B–QB3

And here on 17 . . . PxP; 18 PxP, QxKP; 19 N–B5! is decisive.

18	NxB	PxN
19	R–R3!	P–Q4
20	B–Q3	Q–R2
21	Q–K2!	N–B2
22	P–B5!	. . . .

White's attack steadily builds up in intensity.

22	. . . .	KPxP
23	BxBP!	N–K3

White's Bishop is immune, for if 23 . . . PxB; 24 Q–R5 and White wins.

24	Q–N4	Q–Q2
25	R–KB1	K–N2

BLACK

WHITE

Position after 25 . . . K–N2

26	B–Q3!	. . . .

Black cannot prevent the following sacrifice.

26	. . . .	P–QB4

Black's despair is justified, for even after 26 . . . R–KR1 the continuation would be 27 B–B1! threatening 28 RxRPch!!, RxR; 29 RxPch!!, KxR; 30 QxPch, K–B1; 31 QxR, and White wins.

27	RxRPch!!	Resigns

For after 27 . . . KxR White wins with 28 RxPch!!, RxR; 29 QxPch, K–R1; 30 QxR etc. Black saw everything too late.

THE WEAKER SEX

Since women have been progressing so rapidly in other fields it is surprising that they still have made comparatively little progress as first-class chess players. Miss Menchik was the best to date, and she had some fine wins to her credit; but she was very far from being in the top rank.

DUTCH DEFENSE

Lodz, 1938

WHITE (*J. Gerstenfeld*)   BLACK (*V. Menchik*)

1	P–QB4	P–KB4
2	N–QB3	N–KB3
3	P–KN3	P–K3
4	B–N2	B–K2
5	P–Q4	Castles
6	N–B3	P–Q4

The "Stonewall" formation, which, for all its apparent solidity, can turn out to be pretty shaky.

7	Castles	P–B3
8	B–B4	Q–K1
9	N–K5	Q–R4

The Queen accomplishes nothing of any value here. Consequently 9 . . . N–R4 seems more to the point.

10	P–B3	P–KN4
11	B–B1	QN–Q2
12	Q–B2	NxN
13	PxN	N–Q2
14	PxP	KPxP

After 14 . . . NxKP; 15 PxBP, NxQBP, White opens up the position favorably with 16 P–K4!

15	P–B4	P–N5
16	B–K3	Q–N3

Black sees that 16 . . . B–B4 or 16 . . . N–B4 can be answered favorably with 17 NxP! But 16 . . . N–N3 followed by 17 . . . B–K3 is a more solid alternative.

17	QR–Q1!	P–KR4?
18	B–Q4	R–Q1

White is now ready for a far-reaching combination that shows sensitive evaluation of the possibilities.

BLACK

WHITE

Position after 18 . . . R–Q1

19	BxPch!	PxB
20	NxP	B–B1

Or 20 . . . K–B1; 21 N–B7, R–N1; 22 BxP and Black's menaced Rook has no escape. On 20 . . . Q–R2, White has 21 QxP!

21	P–K6!	QxP

For after 21 . . . N–N3; 22 N–B6ch is too strong.

22	N–B7	Q–QB3
23	QxP!	N–B3

And now 23 . . . QxN?; 24 Q–N6ch and mate next move.

24	Q–N5ch!	K–B2

Black is paying a heavy price for his wanton weakening of the King-side. If 24 . . . B–N2; 25 BxN, QxB; 26 RxRch etc.

25	QxNch!	QxQ
26	BxQ	B–B4ch
27	K–N2!	B–Q2
28	BxR!	. . . .

But not 28 NxR??, B–B3ch and Black wins.

28	. . . .	B–B3ch
29	N–Q5	RxB
30	P–K4	Resigns

Black has no compensation for his lost material. A beautifully engineered attack by White.

THE OLD ORDER CHANGETH

Despite chronic complaint that old-time brilliancy is sadly missing from modern chess, the literature is steadily enriched by beautiful games such as this one.

RUY LOPEZ

Boston, 1938

WHITE (*I. Horowitz*) BLACK (*R. Martin*)

1	P–K4	P–K4
2	N–KB3	N–QB3
3	B–N5	P–QR3
4	B–R4	N–B3
5	Castles	B–K2
6	Q–K2	P–Q3
7	P–B3	B–Q2

Black's ultra-solid defensive formation has the one potential drawback that it may condemn him to an excessively passive position. He will therefore be well advised to use caution in moderation.

8	P–Q4	Castles
9	B–B2	Q–K1

Here, for example, Black misses a splendid opportunity to free himself with 9 . . . PxP!; 10 PxP, N–QN5!; 11 B–N3, B–N4; 12 B–QB4, BxB; 13 QxB, P–Q4!—or 10 NxP, NxN; 11 PxN, B–N4; 12 B–Q3, BxB; 13 QxB, P–Q4; 14 P–K5, N–K5 etc.

10	P–KR3	R–Q1
11	R–K1	K–R1
12	QN–Q2	N–KN1

Hedgehog chess.

13	N–B1	B–B3
14	Q–Q1	QN–K2
15	N–K3	P–B4
16	N–N4!	BxN

He parts with his better Bishop in order to retain his inferior Bishop.

17	PxB	N–B3
18	P–Q5	. . . .

Now that White contemplates forceful action on the newly opened King Rook file, he blocks any diversionary action in the center.

	18	. . . .	N–N1
	19	P–KN3	Q–Q2
	20	P–N5	B–K2
	21	N–R4	P–KN3

Black prevents Q–R5 or N–B5—or so he thinks.

	22	K–N2	P–B3
	23	R–R1	. . . .

The open file comes to life. White threatens 24 NxPch. On 23 . . .
Q–K1; 24 Q–N4 is quite strong.

	23	. . . .	K–N2

BLACK

WHITE

Position after 23 . . . K–N2

	24	N–B5ch!!	PxN

Refusal of the Greek gift is no better: 24 . . . K–R1; 25 RxPch!!,
KxR; 26 Q–R1ch and White wins.

	25	RxPch!!	KxR
	26	Q–R5ch	N–R3

If 26 . . . K–N2; 27 P–N6 is crushing.

	27	QxNch	K–N1
	28	Q–N6ch	K–R1
	29	B–K3	Resigns

The elegant concluding combination has its inner logic as the appropriate culmination of White's encirclement strategy.

AT LEAST 57 VARIETIES

It is interesting to compare this game with Spielmann's effort against Elyashov (page 197), played thirty-five years earlier. We see here that Spielmann's famous attacking style, spiced with at least 57 varieties of complicated tactical sauces, was still turning out a product of high if unpredictable excellence.

KING'S GAMBIT DECLINED

Prague, 1938

WHITE (*R. Spielmann*)   BLACK (*K. Treybal*)

1	P–K4	P–K4
2	P–KB4	B–B4
3	N–KB3	P–Q3
4	P–B3	P–B4

This stab at the center is met energetically by White.

5	BPxP	QPxP
6	P–Q4	KPxP
7	B–QB4	N–KB3
8	P–K5	N–K5
9	PxP	B–N5ch
10	B–Q2	NxB
11	QNxN	N–B3
12	P–Q5!	. . . .

Another tricky move. If now 12 . . . N–K2?; 13 Q–R4ch wins Black's King Bishop. Black fights back ingeniously, but he is doomed to succumb to the power of White's center Pawns.

12	. . . .	P–QN4!
13	B–N3	N–Q5!

For if 14 NxN, Q–R5ch etc.

14	Castles!	B–B4
15	NxN!	. . . .

This involves a Pawn sacrifice which Black at first rejects and then accepts.

15	. . . .	BxNch
16	K–R1	Castles
17	N–B3!	BxNP
18	QR–N1	B–B6

19	Q–K2	Q–K1
20	P–K6	. . . .

With the terrible menace of 21 P–Q6 (threatening P–Q7 or P–K7 dis ch). Now that White has a real Pawn-roller in the center, it is high time for Black's King to depart from the dangerous diagonal; but the removal is only temporary.

20	. . . .	K–R1
21	N–K5	R–B3
22	N–B7ch	K–N1
23	Q–Q3	P–N5
24	RxP	B–R3

BLACK

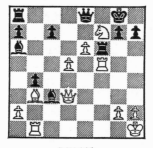

WHITE

Position after 24 . . . B–R3

25	QxB/R6!	. . . .

This well-thought-out sacrifice of the Exchange soon breaks Black's resistance.

25	. . . .	RxR
26	P–Q6	P–N3

If instead 26 . . . PxP; 27 NxP, Q–N3; 28 P–K7 dis ch, K–R1; 29 N–B7ch!, RxN; 30 QxQ, PxQ; 31 BxR, and White wins the other Rook as well.

27	P–Q7	Q–K2

Or 27 . . . Q–KB1 when 28 P–Q8/Q wins at least a Rook.

28	Q–B8ch!	Resigns

For if 28 . . . Q–B1; 29 P–K7 is crushing. The triumph of White's Pawn-roller.

THE FOUR MUSKETEERS

The average player rarely realizes how closely linked strategy and tactics are. White's establishment of a powerful Pawn center is the preliminary to a crushing attack based on the strength of White's Pawns—"the Four Musketeers."

GRUENFELD DEFENSE

Paris, 1940

WHITE (*S. Tartakover*)	BLACK (*E. Znosko-Borovsky*)
1 P–Q4	N–KB3
2 P–QB4	P–KN3
3 N–QB3	P–Q4
4 N–B3	B–N2
5 Q–N3	PxP
6 QxBP	Castles
7 P–K4	P–B3

Too passive. Having surrendered control of the center with his fifth move, Black is committed to active play with his pieces. Hence 7 . . . B–N5 is more appropriate—or perhaps 7 . . . N–R3 followed by 8 . . . P–QB4.

8 B–K2	B–K3
9 Q–Q3	N–R3
10 Castles	P–R3
11 P–KR3	. . . .

There is a significant difference between the moves of the two King Rook Pawns: White's P–KR3 prevents a simplifying exchange by . . . B–N5; Black's . . . P–KR3 is merely a weakening of his castled position.

11	Q–Q2
12 B–K3	QR–Q1

Black's pieces are badly huddled together. His hope of pressure on White's Queen Pawn is quite illusory.

13 Q–Q2	K–R2
14 QR–Q1	N–B2
15 N–K5	Q–B1
16 P–B4	N/B2–K1
17 P–KN4!	. . . .

"The Four Musketeers"—thus spake Tartakover—proceed to demolish Black's position.

17	. . . .	N–Q3
18	Q–B2!	B–Q2
19	NxB	NxN
20	P–K5	N–K1
21	P–B5	P–B4

This comes much too late to do any good.

22	BPxPch	PxNP

White is now ready for a Queen sacrifice which has been well prepared by his previous play.

BLACK

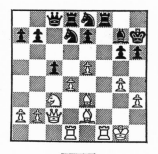

WHITE

Position after 22 . . . PxNP

23	QxPch!!	K–N1

For if 23 . . . KxQ; 24 B–Q3ch, R–B4; 25 BxRch, K–B2; 26 BxN dis ch leaves White a Rook ahead. If 23 . . . K–R1; 24 B–Q3 wins at once.

24	B–QB4ch	P–K3
25	QxKPch	K–R1

Equally disastrous is 25 . . . K–R2; 26 B–Q3ch, K–R1; 27 Q–N6 etc.

26	RxRch	Resigns

For if 26 . . . BxR; 27 Q–N8 mate. A very instructive example of the conversion of positional advantage into crushing attack.

WEAK SQUARES

This concept plays a very important role in modern strategy. It refers to squares that are inadequately protected by one's Pawns. In the following game Black's black squares are weakened by the combination of 13 . . . P–KN3 and the disappearance of Black's protective King Bishop on move 17. White's exploitation of this weakness is really masterful.

NIMZOVICH DEFENSE

Canadian Championship, 1943

	WHITE (*D. Yanofsky*)	BLACK (*J. Therien*)
1	P–K4	N–QB3
2	P–Q4	P–Q4
3	P–K5	B–B4
4	P–QB3	P–K3
5	N–K2	. . . .

More promising than 5 N–B3, as White reserves the possibility of advancing P–KB4–5 after eliminating Black's Queen Bishop.

5	. . . .	KN–K2
6	N–N3	B–N3
7	B–Q3	BxB
8	QxB	N–N3

Hereabouts Black should play . . . Q–Q2 followed by castling Queen-side.

9	P–KB4	B–K2
10	Castles	Castles

This gives Black a rather lifeless game.

11	N–Q2	N–R5
12	N–B3	NxNch

This eases the formation of White's attacking setup. 12 . . . Q–Q2 would have gained some time.

13	RxN	P–KN3

To stop P–B5—but it doesn't.

(*See Diagram on page 250*)

14	P–B5!!	KPxP
15	B–R6!	R–K1
16	NxP!	B–B1

BLACK

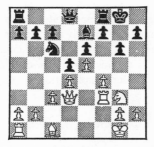

WHITE

Position after 13 . . . P–KN3

For if 16 . . . PxN; 17 R–N3ch, K–R1; 18 B–N7ch, K–N1; 19 B–B6 dis ch, K–B1; 20 R–N8ch!, KxR; 21 Q–N3ch and mate follows. But with the disappearance of his valuable Bishop his black squares become a convenient target for invasion.

17	BxB	RxB
18	N–R6ch	K–N2
19	N–N4	N–K2
20	N–B6	. . . .

Now that White has a decisive grip on the black squares, he systematically strengthens his attacking power.

20	. . . .	P–B3
21	Q–Q2	P–KR3
22	QR–KB1	Q–B1
23	Q–B4	Q–K3
24	Q–N3	QR–Q1

The move White needs to demolish Black's game is P–K6. This is now his objective.

25	N–R5ch	K–N1
26	R–B6	Q–B1
27	P–K6!	Q–N1

If 27 . . . PxP; 28 RxNPch! is deadly.

| 28 | RxBP | Resigns |

Or 28 . . . RxR; 29 RxR, QxQ; 30 N–B6ch, K–R1; 31 R–R7 mate. White's clever Knight play was a notable feature of the winning process.

POSITIONAL ODDS

In the old days, the better player gave his opponent odds by removing one or more of his men from the board. Today a strong player may give odds by burdening himself with a positional weakness which gives him strong theoretical chances of losing the game. In this game White takes upon himself the onus of the doubled and isolated Queen Bishop Pawns. He does not seem unduly troubled, however.

SICILIAN DEFENSE

Zagreb, 1946

WHITE (*B. Rabar*) BLACK (*Tekavchich*)

1	P–K4	P–QB4
2	N–KB3	P–K3
3	P–Q4	PxP
4	NxP	N–KB3
5	N–QB3	B–N5
6	P–K5	. . . .

If White protects his King Pawn with 6 B–Q3, Black gets a fine game with 6 . . . P–Q4. So White understandably prefers to chance the weak Pawn structure that now arises.

6	. . . .	N–Q4
7	B–Q2	NxN
8	PxN	B–K2
9	Q–N4	K–B1

Black temporarily avoids weakening his position with . . . P–KN3.

10	B–Q3	. . . .

White has come out of the opening with a notably aggressive position.

10	. . . .	P–Q3
11	P–KB4	N–Q2
12	Castles	P–KN3

If 12 . . . PxP; 13 NxPch!, PxN; 14 PxP dis ch and White has a virulent attack for the sacrificed piece.

13	QR–K1	N–B4

Encouraged by the fact that there is no communication between Black's Rooks, White now begins a violent attack.

(*See Diagram on page 252*)

BLACK

WHITE

Position after 13 . . . N–B4

14 P–B5!!   . . . .

The decisive break-through on the King Bishop file.

14	. . . .	P–KR4
15	Q–B3	NPxP
16	BxP!	PxB
17	NxP	B–K3

The alternative was 17 . . . BxN; 18 QxB, Q–K1; 19 PxP and White wins.

18	PxP	BxQP
19	RxB!	NxR

Or 19 . . . BxPch; 20 KxB, NxR; 21 B–R6ch and White has a winning attack.

20	NxB	P–B3
21	N–K4!	K–K2
22	B–N5!	. . . .

Beautiful! If 22 . . . PxB; 23 Q–B7 mate. If 22 . . . NxB; 23 QxPch and White wins Queen or Rook.

22	. . . .	Q–N3ch
23	B–K3	Q–Q1

On 23 . . . Q–B3, White sweeps along victoriously with 24 QxPch, K–Q2; 25 N–B5ch! etc.

24	QxPch	K–Q2
25	R–Q1ch	Resigns

An elegant game.

THE NEW ECLECTICISM

During the period 1920–40 there was vast contempt for the old-time openings, particularly the gambits. Since then we have seen a marked revival of these once-despised openings and much midnight oil has been lavished on them.

EVANS GAMBIT

Prague, 1947

WHITE (*V. Pachman*)	BLACK (*Weber*)
1 P–K4	P–K4
2 N–KB3	N–QB3
3 B–B4	B–B4
4 P–QN4	BxNP
5 P–B3	B–R4
6 P–Q4	PxP
7 Castles	P–Q3
8 PxP	B–N3
9 Q–N3?	. . . .

White has not done his homework. The right way is 9 N–B3 (page 184).

| 9 . . . . | B–K3? |

The wrong reply. Correct was 9 . . . N–R4!, for if 10 BxPch?, K–B1; 11 Q–Q5, N–NB3 wins for Black.

10 P–Q5	N–R4
11 Q–B3!	NxB
12 PxB	N–K4
13 NxN	PxN
14 PxPch	KxP

Black hopes to deflect White from his terrific attack: 15 QxKP?, B–Q5; 16 Q–KB5ch, N–B3; 17 R–Q1, BxPch! etc.

15 Q–N3ch!	K–K1
16 N–B3	P–B3
17 B–R3	Q–B3
18 QR–Q1	R–Q1
19 RxRch	KxR

Or 19 . . . QxR; 20 Q–K6ch, N–K2; 21 B–Q6 with a winning

game for White. Black is lost in any event—his King has no haven
and his King-side is undeveloped.

	20	N–R4!	K–B2
	21	B–B5!	BxB
	22	NxB	P–QN3

BLACK

WHITE

Position after 22 . . . P–QN3

With an extra Rook at his disposal, White now decides the game
quickly.

	23	R–Q1!!	PxN
	24	Q–R4	K–N3

Note that 24 . . . K–N1; 25 R–Q7! leads to mate, as does 24 . . .
Q–K3; 25 QxRPch, K–B1; 26 Q–R8ch, K–B2; 27 Q–Q8ch, K–N2;
28 R–N1ch etc.

	25	R–N1ch	K–B2
	26	QxRPch	Resigns

White mates in two more moves. The final phase is distinguished
for its simplicity.

PREMATURE ACTIVITY

The primers for tyros abound in warnings against Black's premature attempts to take the initiative. Yet even outstanding masters are foolish enough to ignore these sound admonitions. The dire results speak for themselves.

SICILIAN DEFENSE

Stockholm, 1948

WHITE (*I. Boleslavsky*)   BLACK (*E. Book*)

1	P–K4	P–QB4
2	N–KB3	P–Q3
3	P–Q4	PxP
4	NxP	N–KB3
5	N–QB3	P–K3
6	B–K2	P–QR3
7	Castles	Q–B2
8	P–B4	N–B3

Black's formation is already familiar to us from page 239.

9	B–K3	B–K2
10	Q–K1	. . . .

White's Queen heads for her most effective square (King Knight 3).

10	. . . .	NxN

This questionable exchange is a preliminary to Black's following, even more dubious move.

11	BxN	P–K4?

Premature. White's refutation is impressive.

12	PxP	PxP
13	Q–N3!	B–B4
14	BxB	QxBch
15	K–R1	K–B1

Black can neither castle nor play 15 . . . KR–N1? because of 16 RxN etc.

(*See Diagram on page 256*)

16	N–Q5!!	NxP

Here 16 . . . QxP?? would be a terrible blunder because of 17 Q–QR3ch, K–N1; 18 N–K7ch leading to a quick mate. Or if 16 . . . NxN; 17 QxKP, QxP??; 18 QxN, Q–B2; 19 RxPch! wins.

BLACK

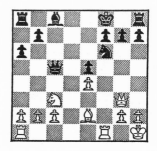

WHITE

Position after 15 . . . K–B1

17	QxKP	N–B3
18	QR–Q1	B–K3

But not 18 . . . NxN; 19 RxPch!! etc.

19	P–QN4!	Q–B3

Again if 19 . . . QxBP??; 20 Q–Q6ch to be followed by smothered mate.

20	NxN	PxN
21	RxP	. . . .

White threatens 22 RxB.

21	. . . .	KR–N1

Black threatens mate.

22	B–B3	Q–N3
23	R–Q6	Q–B7

Again Black threatens mate. (If 23 . . . Q–B2; 24 QRxB!)

24	BxP	QxBP

Another mate threat!

25	QRxB!	Resigns

White operated with notable economy of means.

VULNERABLE DIAGONAL

White's position is dependent on the effectiveness of his fianchettoed King Bishop, which aims at the center and the Queen-side. Yet he soon develops an irresistible King-side attack, and in the last analysis Black collapses because he is vulnerable on the long diagonal.

QUEEN'S PAWN OPENING

Stockholm, 1948

WHITE (*Z. Nilsson*) BLACK (*E. Lundin*)

1	P-Q4	N-KB3
2	N-KB3	P-K3
3	P-B4	B-N5ch
4	B-Q2	Q-K2
5	N-B3	Castles
6	P-KN3	P-B4?

This is inferior to 6 . . . BxN followed by 7 . . . P-QN3 etc. Black's subsequent difficulties are traceable to his difficulties along the neglected long diagonal.

7	B-N2	PxP
8	NxP	N-B3

On 8 . . . Q-B4 White has a more than adequate reply in 9 Q-N3.

9	N-B2!	B-B4
10	Castles	P-QN3?

Too soon—or too late.

(*See Diagram on page 258*)

11	P-QN4!	BxNP

Black has no choice, for if the Bishop retreats, 11 P-N5 is decisive.

12	NxB	QxN
13	N-Q5!	QxP

If 13 . . . Q-Q3 White has a neat winning reply in 14 B-N4!

14	NxNch	PxN
15	B-R6	R-K1

This enables White to carry out a neat combination, but after 15 . . . R-Q1 there follows 16 R-B1, Q-N4; 17 BxN and White wins.

16	R-B1!	Q-KN5
17	RxN!	PxR
18	BxP	B-R3
19	BxKR	RxB

BLACK

WHITE

Position after 10 . . . P–QN3?

Or 19 . . . BxP; 20 Q–Q7, Q–N3; 21 R–K1 and White is a piece to the good.

20	Q–Q7	R–R1
21	R–Q1!	. . . .

White threatens 22 Q–Q8ch! etc.

21	. . . .	Resigns

For if 21 . . . K–R1; 22 Q–K7! wins. Drastic and neat!

LITTLE SINS, BIG PAY-OFF

To most players Black's sins may seem trifling. But the punishment, when it comes, is drastic indeed.

DUTCH DEFENSE

Venice, 1948

WHITE (*M. Najdorf*)   BLACK (*H. Grob*)

1	P–Q4	P–K3
2	P–QB4	P–KB4
3	P–KN3	N–KB3
4	B–N2	B–N5ch
5	B–Q2	BxBch

This exchange is perfectly acceptable if Black means to play . . . P–Q3 and . . . P–K4 later on.

6	QxB	Castles
7	N–QB3	P–Q4

With this and his next move Black sets up the Stonewall formation. But the wall will be rather shaky, his black squares being weak because of the earlier exchange of his King Bishop.

8	N–B3	P–B3
9	Castles	QN–Q2
10	P–K3	PxP?

To win a Pawn, he ruins his Stonewall formation. The results are grievous. White's play throughout is admirable.

11	Q–K2	P–QN4
12	N–N5!	N–N1
13	P–KR4	. . . .

White avoids 13 NxNP? which would cost him a piece after 13 . . . N–Q4!

13	. . . .	P–KR3
14	N–R3!	N–Q4
15	P–K4!	. . . .

White plays consistently to open new lines.

15	. . . .	NxN
16	PxN	P–QR4
17	N–B4	K–R2
18	KR–K1!	R–R2
19	P–R5!	Q–B2

While White has built up formidable pressure, Black is still trying to uncork his pieces.

20	PxP!	PxP
21	P–Q5!	R–Q1
22	QR–Q1	P–B4

Black tries to keep the position closed, but White insists on opening it.

(*See Diagram on page 260*)

23	P–Q6!!	RxP
24	B–Q5!	. . . .

White threatens 25 B–N8ch!, KxB; 26 Q–K8ch, K–R2; 27 Q–N6ch!, RxQ; 28 PxRch and 29 R–K8 mate.

24	. . . .	Q–Q1

Or 24 . . . R–Q1 when 25 Q–K8!!, RxQ; 26 RxR, P–N4; 27 PxP *e.p.* ch, K–N2; 28 B–B7! is disastrous for Black.

25	Q–K8	. . . .

BLACK

WHITE

Position after 22 . . . P–B4

White threatens mate beginning with 26 B–N8ch etc. Black's reply is sheer despair.

| 25 | . . . . | B–K3 |
| 26 | RxB | Resigns |

Admirably played by White.

MODERN TREND

We have already noticed (pages 180, 255, and 260) that the modern master is apt to be quite brutal in his treatment of the Sicilian Defense. Here is still another example, in which White makes it all seem so deceptively effortless.

Sicilian Defense

Zagreb, 1948

	white (B. Rabar)	black (Vukovich)
1	P–K4	P–QB4
2	N–KB3	N–QB3
3	P–Q4	PxP
4	NxP	N–B3
5	N–QB3	P–Q3
6	B–K2	P–K3
7	Castles	B–K2

	8	B–K3	Castles
	9	P–B4	P–QR3

The Scheveningen Variation, which, as we have seen, leads to highly critical positions.

	10	B–B3	Q–B2
	11	N–N3	N–QR4
	12	NxN	QxN
	13	Q–K1!	Q–B2

White was threatening to get a considerable positional advantage with 14 N–Q5!, eliminating Black's valuable King Bishop.

	14	K–R1	B–Q2
	15	Q–N3!	K–R1
	16	B–Q4!	. . . .

The right diagonal for this Bishop.

	16	. . . .	N–K1
	17	QR–Q1	R–B1
	18	P–B5!	P–QN4

Black sees that 18 . . . P–K4 will not do, for then 19 N–Q5 is killing.

	19	P–QR3	P–QR4
	20	PxP	PxP
	21	B–K2!	. . . .

With impeccable judgment White foresees that the game is to be decided on the King Bishop file.

	21	. . . .	P–N5
	22	RxRch	BxR
	23	R–KB1!	K–N1

(*See Diagram on page 262*)

	24	B–R5!	PxN

Declining the sacrifice is no better, for example 24 . . . P–N3; 25 BxP!, PxB; 26 QxPch, B–N2; 27 R–B7 and White wins—or 26 . . . N–N2; 27 RxBch! with the same result.

	25	B–B7ch!	K–R1
	26	BxN	K–N1

Here too, if 26 . . . RxB; 27 RxBch! etc.

	27	Q–B2!	Resigns

The finish might have been 27 . . . RxB; 28 Q–B7ch, K–R1; 29 QxBch and mate next move. White's incisive preparations for the attack led to a fine finish.

BLACK

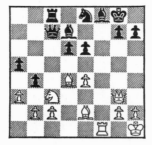

WHITE

Position after 23 . . . K–N1

PLAYING BY THE BOOK

Some players are reassured by playing book variations and relying on authority. But sometimes, as in the following game, the results are anything but reassuring.

QUEEN'S GAMBIT DECLINED

Trencianske Teplice, 1949

WHITE (*G. Stahlberg*)   BLACK (*J. Sefc*)

1	P–QB4	N–KB3
2	P–Q4	P–K3
3	N–KB3	P–Q4

By transposition the players have reached the Queen's Gambit Declined.

4	B–N5	B–N5ch
5	N–B3	PxP
6	P–K4	P–B4
7	BxP	PxP
8	NxP	Q–R4

This counterattack looks very powerful, but White has surprisingly effective resources.

9	BxN!	BxNch

10	PxB!	QxBPch?
11	K–B1	QxBch

White seems hopelessly lost, but there is much more here than meets the eye.

| 12 | K–N1 | . . . . |

Now Black must not play 12 . . . PxB? because of 13 R–B1 and White wins. Likewise 12 . . . B–Q2? is not good because of 13 R–B1, Q–R3; 14 NxP! with decisive advantage for White.

12	. . . .	N–Q2
13	BxP	KR–N1
14	R–B1	Q–R3
15	B–R6	N–B3

Or 15 . . . N–K4; 16 Q–R5, N–Q6; 17 N–N5! and White wins.

16	P–K5!	N–Q4
17	P–KR4!!	B–Q2
18	Q–B2!	R–N3

Obviously 18 . . . QR–B1 will not do because of 19 QxRch, when White gets too much material for his Queen.

BLACK

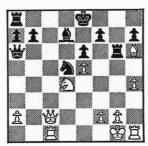

WHITE

Position after 18 . . . R–N3

| 19 | P–R5!! | R–N5 |

Curiously 19 . . . RxB fails because of 20 Q–Q2, and Black's unfortunate Rook cannot escape. And if 19 . . . R–B1; 20 QxRch, BxQ; 21 RxBch, K–Q2; 22 PxR, KxR; 23 PxRP wins for White.

20	QxP	K–K2
21	R–R4!	R/N5–N1

Not 21 . . . RxR; 22 B–N5ch and White forces mate.

22	B–N7	Q–R6
23	B–B6ch	K–B1
24	R–B7!!	NxB

The alternative 24 . . . NxR is refuted by 25 P–R6! and Black has no good reply to the threat of 26 QxRch!, KxQ; 27 P–R7ch, K–B1; 28 P–R8/Q mate.

25	PxN	Q–Q3
26	P–R6!	Resigns

Black is helpless against Q–N7ch! etc. White's play was a triumph of exquisite artistry.

QUEEN'S ABDICATION

To send the Queen on a menial errand is always courting danger. This is especially true when—as here—one's opponent is in a position to work up a powerful attack.

QUEEN'S GAMBIT DECLINED

Belgrade, 1950

WHITE (*S. Tordion*)   BLACK (*C. Hugot*)

1	P–QB4	N–KB3
2	N–QB3	P–K3
3	P–Q4	P–Q4

As in the previous game, a Queen's Gambit Declined has been arrived at by devious ways.

4	B–N5	B–K2
5	P–K3	Castles
6	N–B3	QN–Q2
7	R–B1	P–QR3
8	PxP	PxP

The Exchange Variation, in which White's future depends on Queen-side operations, while Black has some nebulous possibilities of King-side attack.

9	B–Q3	R–K1
10	Castles	P–B3
11	Q–B2	N–B1

12 Q–N1   . . . .

While this move is not inevitably fatal, it certainly points to such
a possibility. White wants to play P–QN4–5 to develop a Queen-side
initiative; but R–N1 was surely a more economical way to begin.

12 . . . .   N–K5
13 BxB   QxB
14 BxN   PxB
15 N–Q2   B–B4

After the foregoing exchanges Black's attacking stock has begun
to rise appreciably. White would therefore have been well-advised to
play 16 P–B4!, opening up good defensive possibilities on the second
rank.

16 P–QN4   QR–Q1
17 N–B4?   . . . .

Intended to stop . . . R–Q3–R3—but 17 P–B4 was still the move.

17 . . . .   Q–N4!

Black threatens . . . B–R6 and also prevents 18 P–B4, which would
now be refuted by 18 . . . PxP *e.p.* From now on, Black's King-side
possibilities become progressively more menacing.

18 N–K2   N–N3
19 N–N3   N–R5
20 N–QR5   R–K3!
21 NxNP   . . . .

BLACK

WHITE

Position after 21 NxNP

21 . . . .   R–R3!!

Black has in his mind's eye the following: 22 NxR, N–B6ch!; 23

PxN, Q–R5; 24 KR–Q1, QxPch; 25 K–B1, PxP!!; 26 QxB, Q–R8ch!; 27 NxQ, RxN mate!

| | 22 | P–B4 | . . . . |

Losing quickly, but also after 22 KR–Q1, R–Q4 Black has a winning attack.

22	. . . .	PxP *e.p.*
23	P–K4	Q–K6ch
24	R–B2	PxP!
	Resigns	

And quite rightly so, for after White captures the Bishop the reply 24 . . . N–B6ch is murderous.

NO CONVICTION

As we study this game it becomes apparent that Black has no real faith in the defense he has adopted. White senses this lack of conviction and exploits the situation in an appropriately aggressive spirit.

QUEEN'S GAMBIT DECLINED

Buenos Aires, 1955

WHITE (*L. Szabo*)	BLACK (*A. Bisguier*)
1 P–Q4	P–Q4
2 P–QB4	P–QB3
3 N–KB3	N–B3
4 N–B3	P–K3
5 P–K3	QN–Q2
6 B–Q3	B–Q3
7 P–K4	. . . .

White's best chance of seizing the initiative.

7	PxKP
8 NxP	NxN
9 BxN	N–B3

If Black wants to equalize—and that is all he has a right to hope for—then 9 . . . P–K4 is his best chance.

| 10 B–B2 | B–N5ch |

Black plays for simplification—a plausible thought but not good enough.

11	B–Q2	BxBch
12	QxB	Castles
13	N–K5!	. . . .

White posts his Knight powerfully, at the same time temporarily preventing . . . P–QN3—the move Black needs for developing his Bishop.

13	. . . .	Q–B2
14	Castles/Q!	. . . .

Ordinarily this is very dangerous in Queen Pawn openings. Not so here, as Black lacks the slightest chance for counterattack.

14	. . . .	P–B4
15	Q–K3!	P–QN3
16	PxP	PxP

This mode of recapture is dictated by Black's desire to prevent the aggressive maneuver R–Q4–R4. But White has other ways of forcing the attack.

BLACK

WHITE

Position 16 . . . PxP

17	P–KN4!	. . . .

This bayonet thrust is decisive, for example 17 . . . B–N2; 18 P–N5!, N–K1 (not 18 . . . BxR; 19 PxN, B–N2; 20 Q–N5, P–N3; 21 Q–R6 forcing mate); 19 KR–N1 (19 R–Q7 should also win, but in a much more complicated manner), and White has an easy win as in the actual continuation.

17	. . . .	R–N1
18	KR–N1	Q–N3

A forlorn hope.

19	P–N3	R–N2
20	P–N5	N–K1

Here 20 . . . N–Q2 looks like the indicated move, but to no avail: 21 RxN!, RxR; 22 NxR, BxN; 23 Q–Q3 and the mate threat wins Black's Bishop. Or 21 . . . BxR; 22 Q–Q3, R–Q1 (if 22 . . . P–N3; 23 NxB wins for White); 23 QxPch, K–B1; 24 Q–R8ch, K–K2; 25 QxP and White wins with ease.

21	BxPch!	KxB
22	Q–R3ch	K–N1
23	R–N4	Resigns

And rightly so. For if 23 . . . P–B3; 24 R–R4, PxN; 25 P–N6 followed by R–R8 mate.

CHILD WONDER

Chess has had several child prodigies. The latest of them is Bobby Fischer, who in many ways shows the poise and *savoir faire* of much older players.

SICILIAN DEFENSE

Portoroz, 1959

WHITE (*R. Fischer*)	BLACK (*B. Larsen*)
1	P–K4	P–QB4
2	N–KB3	P–Q3
3	P–Q4	PxP
4	NxP	N–KB3
5	N–QB3	P–KN3
6	B–K3	B–N2
7	P–B3	. . . .

White prevents . . . N–KN5 before proceeding with Q–Q2 and B–QB4.

7	. . . .	Castles
8	Q–Q2	N–B3
9	B–QB4	NxN
10	BxN	B–K3

Black wants to neutralize the strength of White's well-placed King Bishop.

| 11 | B–N3 | Q–R4 |
| 12 | Castles/Q | P–QN4 |

Black can build a more tenacious defense with 12 . . . BxB.

13	K–N1	P–N5
14	N–Q5	BxN
15	BxB	QR–B1

Black realizes that after 15 . . . NxB; 16 BxB, KxB; 17 PxN, White has two attacking possibilities: P–KR4–5 opening the King Rook file, as well as doubling Rooks on the King file to press on Black's backward King Pawn.

16	B–N3	R–B2
17	P–KR4	Q–N4
18	P–R5!	KR–B1

This effort at counterplay is futile, but 18 . . . NxRP loses even more rapidly, for example 19 BxB, NxB; 20 Q–R6, N–R4; 21 P–N4, N–B3; 22 P–N5, N–R4; 23 RxN, PxR; 24 P–N6, RPxP; 25 QxPch and White has a quick mate.

19	PxP	RPxP
20	P–N4!	P–R4
21	P–N5	N–R4

BLACK

WHITE

Position after 21 . . . N–R4

| 22 | RxN! | . . . . |

Smashing Black's flimsy barricade on the King Rook file. The rather banal sacrifice is redeemed by White's subsequent forceful play.

| 22 | . . . . | PxR |
| 23 | P–N6! | P–K4 |

The subtle point of White's sacrifice is that the seemingly adequate 23 . . . P–K3 is refuted by 24 PxPch, RxP; 25 BxP, while if 24 . . . KxP, White has the decisive 25 Q–B4ch!

24	PxPch	K–B1
25	B–K3	P–Q4
26	PxP	RxKBP
27	P–Q6	R–KB3
28	B–N5!	. . . .

Another important point. The menaced Rook dare not move because of 29 B–K7ch, K–K1; 30 P–Q7ch etc.

28	. . . .	Q–N2
29	BxR	BxB
30	P–Q7	R–Q1

Now the strongest move is 31 Q–R6ch (forcing mate), but the move actually chosen by White is quite satisfactory.

| 31 | Q–Q6ch | Resigns |

For if 31 . . . K–N2; 32 R–N1ch wins easily, while if 31 . . . B–K2; 32 Q–R6 mate.

Boners of the Masters

What? After enjoying the beautiful ideas and profound stratagems of the masters, we are now to survey their blunders and transgressions?! It smacks of the basest ingratitude. Worse yet, it lays us open to a charge of *Schadenfreude*—that marvelously expressive Teutonicism which might be rendered as "malicious rejoicing over somebody else's misfortune."

Far be it from us. These blunders merely prove that the masters are made of common clay like the rest of us. So much the more highly, then, must we value their flights of genius. Besides, the criticisms are not always correct. On these occasions, at least, the master receives poetic justice, if no other kind.

As far as that goes, there are some "mistakes" that once upon a time were considered masterpieces. Undoubtedly this is the most remarkable example:

(*See Diagram 1 on page 272*)

Having played his beloved Evans Gambit, Anderssen is two Pawns and the Exchange down but has a ferocious attack. Black threatens to exchange Queens, and has a secondary threat of . . . Q–Q7 (intending . . . QxP mate).

Here is how Anderssen solved his problem:

1	Q–N5!	Q–Q7!

The mate threat is a fine reply to White's threat of 2 Q–R6. What is more, White can no longer stave off the exchange of Queens.

2	N–B5!!	. . . .

The first point of this wonderful Queen sacrifice is that Black cannot decline it by 2 . . . QxB? because of 3 N–K7ch, K–R1; 4 RxPch!, KxR; 5 Q–R4 mate.

2	. . . .	QxQ
3	N–K7ch	K–R1

Has White blundered? Definitely not.

ANDERSSEN–ZUKERTORT
Breslau, 1862

BLACK

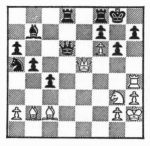

WHITE

1. *White to play*

    4 NxPch!   . . . .

Now the second point of the Queen sacrifice appears: Black must give up his Queen, for if 4 . . . PxN; 5 P–B7 dis ch and White forces mate, while if 4 . . . K–N1; 5 N–K7ch, K–R1; 6 RxP mate!

    4 . . . .   QxN!

    5 BxQ   . . . .

Now White threatens to win with 6 RxPch, K–N1; 7 R–N7ch, K–R1; 8 BxP etc.

    5 . . . .   R–Q7!

With the double threat of . . . RxPch as well as . . . RxB. White must be content with a draw.

    6 RxPch   K–N1

    7 R–N7ch   K–R1

    8 R–R7ch   Drawn

White draws by perpetual check.

All very pretty and thoroughly admirable—and yet White has better! Seventy years later Alekhine was shown a diagram of the position (see diagram) and in a few minutes he found Anderssen's drawing line. Still not satisfied, he studied the position a few more minutes and demonstrated a win. Unfortunately Alekhine's moves were not recorded, and nobody knows to this day what his moves were.

About twenty-five years later B. H. Wood, a noted English player and journalist, was asked to reconstruct Alekhine's solution, or at least to make an educated guess as to its nature.

Wood came up with an ingenious solution:

1 BxP!! Here are the possibilities:

2. 1 . . . BPxP; 2 P–B7ch! wins at once.

2. 1 . . . RPxB; 2 Q–N5, Q–Q7; 3 N–B5!, QxQ; 4 N–K7ch, K–R1; 5 RxP mate.

3. 1 . . . QxQ; 2 BxRPch, K–R1; 3 BxQ and White must win. He threatens 4 B–B7 in addition to 4 N–B5 followed by a discovered check that forces mate.

Whether or not this was Alekhine's solution, it demotes Anderssen's beautiful sequence to the status of a blunder. But who can describe Anderssen's exquisite play as a blunder? I for one cannot bring myself to such a drastic formulation. So let us turn to an indisputable example of prime stupidity which is simply incredible for two masters of note.

KOSTICH–RUBINSTEIN
Carlsbad, 1911

BLACK

WHITE

2. Black to play

The play was:

1 . . . .   K–K3??

2	N–Q4ch	KxP??
3	NxB??	R–N7
4	R–B5	K–Q3
5	R–B8	K–Q2

This perpetual pursuit of the White Rook saves Black from defeat.

| 6 | R–B5 | K–Q3 |
| 7 | R–B3 | P–Q5 |

And after 8 R–B4, P–Q6; 9 R–Q4ch, K–K4; 10 RxP, RxNch Black has a draw, as White's extra Pawn is not enough to win in an ending in which all the Pawns are on one side of the board.

All very neat, but how did Black overlook that on 2 . . . KxP?? White could play 3 N–B6ch forking King and Rook? And how did White overlook this as well?!

But it would never do to be supercilious about such happenings in a great master tournament. Strain, fatigue, and time pressure play many a strange trick on the contestants. Take this example from one of the closing rounds of the same grueling tournament:

RUBINSTEIN–CHAJES
Carlsbad, 1911

BLACK

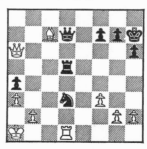

WHITE

3. Black to play

Black has played superbly and can now win easily with:

1   ....   QxB

What could be more obvious?

    2   RxN   Q–B8ch

    3   K–R2   Q–B8

And Black wins a Rook.

Instead, Black played 1 . . . P–B4? and even managed to lose eventually.

There seems to be no end to the aberrations that may arise in the course of a hard-fought game. For example:

FLOHR–GROB
Match, 1932

BLACK

WHITE

4. White to play

In this position Black threatens . . . Q–B8 mate. Seeing no way of escape, White resigned.

Yet he had a defense: 1 K–R1! in order to answer 1 . . . Q–B8ch with 2 B–N1. But in the heat of the battle White simply went to pieces.

Even in the absence of any discernible pressure a player may lose his head. That is what happened in the following easily won position:

(*See Diagram 5 on page 276*)

HOROWITZ–PAVEY
U. S. Championship, 1951

BLACK

WHITE

5. Black to play

With two Pawns and the Exchange ahead, Black must win if he observes a modicum of care. Eager to finish in the simplest manner possible, Black plays:

1	....	QxBch??
2	QxQ	R–R6

Black anticipates 3 K–N2??, RxQ; 4 KxR, P–N6 and the Pawn queens. What could be simpler?

3	K–R4!!	RxQ

Black has no choice—but White is stalemated!

Just as players sometimes resign under a mistaken impression that all is lost, they sometimes give up a won position as drawn. Here is a famous example:

(See Diagram 6 on page 277)

There followed:

1	P–B7	R–R4ch
2	K–N6	R–R3ch!

This maneuver makes life difficult for White. The point is that he cannot play 3 KxR?, for then Black's Pawn queens with a check.

3	K–B5	R–R4ch
4	K–B6	R–R3ch
5	K–Q5	R–R4ch
6	K–K6	R–R3ch

BOGOLYUBOV–THOMAS
Hastings, 1922

BLACK

WHITE

6. White to play

Here White, seeing no way to win, gave the position up as a draw, only to have the following win demonstrated to him:

7	K–Q5	R–R4ch
8	K–B4	R–R5ch
9	K–N3	R–R6ch
10	K–B2	R–QB6ch

Of course Black cannot queen in view of the reply 11 P–B8/Q mate —or even 11 P–B8/R mate.

11	K–N2!	R–B7ch
12	K–R1!	. . . .

The winning position, as Black must now move his Rook, remaining on the Queen Bishop file but allowing White to capture the Black Pawn. White's King then marches down to Queen Knight 7—a lengthy but easy win. Of course, if Black plays 12 . . . K–B1, White wins with 13 P–B8/Qch or 13 R–R8ch—the order doesn't matter.

As pointed out earlier, mistakes committed in the heat of the battle are humanly understandable and excusable. But what are we to say of the mistakes committed under leisurely working conditions in the quiet of the author's study? (Modesty forbids my mentioning some of my own more startling achievements in this field.) When superb masters of the end game—such outstanding men as Lasker and

Capablanca—go wrong in simple endings, then we can only proclaim our utter bafflement.

Here is a simple ending in which Lasker goes sadly wrong:

BLACK

WHITE

7. Black to play

Discussing this position in his *Manual of Chess,* Lasker makes the point that it is difficult to turn a material advantage to account when the Bishops move on squares of different color. Here, he says, is a position which cannot be won even with three Pawns ahead. The play is:

1 . . . .   K–Q5

Threatening to win with . . . P–B6.

2   K–N2   K–K6

Threatening to win with 3 . . . P–Q7. If now 3 K–B3, K–K7; 4 B–Q2, P–N5ch wins for Black.

3   K–B1   . . . .

Now Lasker continues 3 . . . K–K5; 4 B–R5, K–Q4; 5 K–N2, K–B4; 6 K–R3 and Black, foiled at every turn, must apparently concede a draw. But a humble amateur otherwise unknown to fame—one A. Fanderl—shows a neat win for Black:

3 . . . .   P–Q7ch!

4   BxP   K–Q6

And Black wins easily, for example 5 B–N4, P–B6; 6 K–N1, K–B5; 7 B–R3, P–N5; 8 B–B1, P–N6; 9 B–R3, B–N3ch; 10 K–R1, K–Q6; 11 B–R3, K–B7 and White soon will be mated.

In his *Chess Fundamentals* Capablanca says of the following position: "White can't win by 1 P–B5. Black's best answer would be 1 . . . P–N3 draws. (The student should work this out.)"

Capablanca's works are studded with this beguiling phrase, but Dr. Jeno Ban, on taking Capa at his word, made a startling discovery.

BLACK

WHITE

8. *White to play*

| 1 | P–B5 | P–N3 |
| 2 | PxP | K–K3 |

Dr. Ban points out that after 3 K–K4?, K–B3; 4 P–N7, KxP; 5 K–B5, K–B2 the position is a well-known draw. (For example 6 P–N5, K–N2; 7 P–N6, K–N1!; 8 K–B6, K–B1; 9 P–N7ch, K–N1; 10 K–N6, stalemate.) But Dr. Ban shows the position is won for White in the following clever manner:

3	P–N5!	K–K2
4	K–K5!	K–B1
5	K–B6	K–N1
6	P–N7	K–R2
7	P–N8/Qch!	. . . .

Very neat. Note that 7 P–N6ch, K–N1 only draws. As Capablanca would say, the student should work this out.

| 7 | . . . . | KxQ |
| 8 | K–N6 and wins |

For example: 8 . . . K–B1; 9 K–R7 ensures the queening of White's Pawn; likewise after 8 . . . K–R1; 9 K–B7 etc.

But perhaps the prize boner of them all was committed by the great Tarrasch in his comments on the following position:

VIDMAR—TEICHMANN
Carlsbad, 1907

BLACK

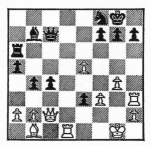

WHITE

9. Black to play

Teichmann, who was blind in one eye but nevertheless had an excellent sight of the board, now played 1 . . . R–KN3. Tarrasch, in his notes to the game, heaps mountains of scorn on poor Teichmann's head, strongly recommends 1 . . . QxP and gives several paragraphs of formidable-looking analysis to prove his point.

However, what Tarrasch overlooks—and what Teichmann saw at the first glance of his one good eye—was that 1 . . . QxP?? allows a beautiful mate in five:

1	. . . .	QxP??
2	QxRPch!!	NxQ
3	R–Q8ch	Q–K1
4	RxQch	N–B1
5	R–R8ch!	KxR
6	RxN mate!	

To draw a moral would be anticlimactic, not to say uncharitable. So, "the rest is silence."

Chess Players All

In all times and places chess players of every degree of skill have displayed certain traits in common. Their passion for the game, their absorption, their rage at losing—these are qualities that turn up from many sources, no matter how disparate they may be. These remarks apply equally well to masters and to tyros. Taken singly, these revealing observations give us a telling glimpse of the unshakable grip in which this unique game holds its devotees. Taken as a whole, these excerpts give us an unsurpassed comment on human nature, its quirks and vagaries.

I have known chess masters who, after a defeat, stayed in their rooms for a whole day, unable to eat or cheer up.

—RICHARD RÉTI

Nothing is so healthy as a thrashing at the proper time, and from few won games have I learned as much as I have from most of my defeats.

—J. R. CAPABLANCA

You cannot play at Chess if you are kindhearted.

—*French Proverb*

In the course of a game at the Argentine Chess Club, Buenos Aires, a well-known player made a move of decisive character. His opponent studied the position some little time, and then said: "That threatens mate."

"Yes, señor, in three moves."

"Then why did you not announce it?"

"Because I didn't see it!"

—*British Chess Magazine,* 1920

In the laboratory the gambits all test unfavorably, but the old rule wears well, that all gambits are sound over the board.

　　　　　　　　　　　　　　　　　　—W. E. NAPIER

In a gambit you give up a Pawn for the sake of getting a lost game.

　　　　　　　　　　　　　　　　　　—SAMUEL BODEN

Of my fifty-seven years I have applied at least thirty to forgetting most of what I had learned or read, and since I succeeded in this I have acquired a certain ease and cheer which I should never again like to be without. If need be, I can increase my skill in chess, if need be I can do that of which I have no idea at present. I have stored little in my memory, but I can apply that little, and it is of good use in many and varied emergencies. I keep it in order, but resist every attempt to increase its dead weight.

　　　　　　　　　　　—EMANUEL LASKER, *Manual of Chess*

I discovered the Rabbi of Puspok playing at chess with Monkey's Arm. It is a forbidden game, because kings, queens, bishops and knights are so many figurative beings, and these harmless figures take on themselves the anathema pronounced by Moses against idols. But a man is not a Talmudist for nothing, and Reb Chapse, carried away by his passion, eluded the difficulty by substituting coins for the chessmen.

　　　　　—JEROME AND JEAN THARAUD, *La Rose de Sâron*

During a Paris tournament once, Baptz asked me if I would pose while he sculptured my head. Feeling greatly flattered, I consented. When I left, he promised to send the result on to Antwerp for me. Next year I met him and asked what had happened to it. "Oh, I sold it to a friend of mine," he answered. "Oh, how nice," I replied, mollified at once; "who was it wanted a bust of me?" "They didn't want a bust of you," he replied, "they wanted one of Alekhine."

　　　　　　　　　　—GEORGE KOLTANOWSKI, *Chess*, 1935

There are many checks, but only one mate.

　　　　　　　　　　　　　　　　　　—*Russian Proverb*

Here are some of the questions and answers to an examination paper in chess that was given some time ago by Dr. Tarrasch. Some of the answers to the questions, though flippant, contain a grain of truth and are, besides, interesting.

Q. What is the object of playing a gambit opening?

A. To acquire a reputation of being a dashing player at the cost of losing a game.

Q. Account briefly for the popularity of the Queen Pawn opening in matches of a serious nature.

A. Laziness.

Q. What is the duty of an umpire where a player wilfully upsets the board?

A. Remove the bottle.

Q. What exceptional circumstances will justify the stopping of clocks during a tournament game?

A. Strangling a photographer.

—Chess Review, 1935

From Anderssen I learned how to make combinations; from Tarrasch I learned how to avoid making them.

—Rudolf Spielmann

Habitués of the old Crosby Hall at luncheon, or later of the Ship and Turtle, will not easily forget his happy smile as a particularly fine trap secured a win in an apparently lost situation. On one occasion, against a player very intent on his attack on one side of the board, he queened a pawn on the other, to lose it to a rook. A spectator silently handed it back to him under the table. The pawn was again queened, and yet a third time, the unsuspecting opponent blandly taking it off each time, far too intent on his attack to detect the deception, which caused much laughter among the onlookers.

—British Chess Magazine, 1920

We have heard of a lady suffering herself to be undressed, without perceiving it, while immersed in the mysterious movements of Queen, Bishops and Knights.

—The Gentleman's Magazine, 1787

. . . A memory of Hastings twenty years ago. Rubinstein is due to play G. M. Norman, but half an hour after the time of commencement, no sign of him. Another half hour passes with his clock ticking merrily against him, when one of the officials looks in at Rubinstein's nearby hotel. The grand master is found peacefully asleep, having forgotten all about his game. Unceremoniously awakened, Rubinstein finds he has only 30 minutes in which to make 40 moves. Result: his *opponent* overstepped the time limit!

—M. E. GOLDSTEIN, *Chess World*, 1946

Place the contents of the chessbox in your hat, shake them up vigorously, pour them on the board at a height of two feet, and you get the style of Steinitz.

—H. E. BIRD

He [Bagueret] bethought himself to propose that I should learn chess, of which he had some knowledge. I had a try, almost in spite of myself, and after learning the moves as well as I could, my progress was so rapid that before the end of the first sitting I gave him the odds of the rook, which at the beginning he had given me. I needed no more. I went frantically mad with chess. I bought *Il Calabrese* [a contemporary treatise on chess]. I shut myself up in my room and spent days and nights there with a will to learn all the games by heart, to cram them into my head willy-nilly, to play alone without end or remission.

After two or three months' working in that fine way, and after unimaginable endeavors, I went to the Café with a lean and sallow face, and nearly stupid. I made a trial, playing with M. Bagueret again. He beat me once, twice, twenty times. My head was all of a muddle with those chess combinations, and my imagination had become so dull that I saw nothing more than a cloud before me.

—JEAN JACQUES ROUSSEAU, *Confessions*, 1782

Just as Rousseau could not compose without having his cat beside him, so I cannot really play chess well without my King Bishop. Without it the game seems lifeless and empty, and I cannot devise any plan of attack.

—SIEGBERT TARRASCH

It is astonishing how much hot water a master can wade into the first dozen moves, despite a century of opening exploration!

—W. E. NAPIER

One of Blackburne's opponents in a simultaneous display ordered himself a pick-me-up. The next time Blackburne arrived at that board, he drained the glass at a draught, made his move and passed on. Asked afterwards how he had managed to beat that man so quickly, he explained: "My opponent left a glass of whisky *en prise* and I took it *en passant*. That little mistake wrecked his game."

—B. H. WOOD, *Illustrated London News*, 1950

In Life we are all duffers.

—EMANUEL LASKER, *Manual of Chess*

Scandal has already smeared baseball, football, and basketball. The only sports we can still trust are chess contests and marble tournaments.

—NEW YORK *Daily News*, 1951

If a man wanted to solve one of Loyd's problems by analyzing every possible move on the board, he would naturally get the solution, but only on his last trial—not before!

—WILHELM STEINITZ

My theory of a key move was always to make it just the reverse of what a player in 999 cases out of 1000 would look for.

—SAM LOYD

Methodical thinking is of more use in chess than inspiration.

—C. J. S. PURDY

Another of my clients at Purssell's was a wealthy City merchant, Mr. Pizzi, an Italian by birth, but naturalized in England. His English was worse than mine, and when a third party interfered in his game, making remarks on a certain move, Mr. Pizzi, very indignantly: "Sir, you must not talk into the chess."

—O. C. MULLER, *British Chess Magazine*, 1932

Chess is a matter of vanity.

—ALEXANDER ALEKHINE, *Chess Review*, 1934

A particular point of attraction for Anderssen proved to be a certain cellar, situated in the heart of Berlin, and the particular magnet there was the youthful and very pretty daughter of the keeper, whose duty it was to serve the sparkling draught to her father's guests. Annie, as was the name of the charming girl, was also a chess player, and not averse to having now and then a game with our professor. The latter was, of course, too chivalrous to win many games, and managed generally to let his lovely adversary get the better of him, although she was, of course, no match for him. But on one occasion she had the temerity to gain two games in succession, which feat elated her to such an extent that she ran excitedly around the room, telling everybody of her remarkable luck. This angered Anderssen. The lion within him had been roused. Annie was checkmated five times in rapid succession, which defeat made her so low-spirited that she sulkily retreated from our table, and for a long time after refused to show herself in the barroom.

—ERNST FALKBEER, *Memoirs*

Chess is as much a mystery as women.

—C. J. S. PURDY

Chess is 99 per cent tactics.

—RICHARD TEICHMANN

As might be anticipated, Napoleon as a chess player was not really of great force. His soul demanded a larger field for the expression of its faculties. His chess was that of Marengo, of Austerlitz, of Jena. Upon our mosaic of 64 squares, I could have given him the rook; upon his own board he could afford the odds to Julius Caesar.

Bonaparte had no time to make chess a study. He played the openings badly, and was impatient if his adversary dwelt too long upon his move. Every minute of the clock was life to a mind so energetic. In the middle stage of the game, when the skirmish was really complicated of aspect, Napoleon frequently struck out a brilliant *coup*. Under defeat at chess, the great soldier was sore and irritable; although it was presumed that those favorites with whom he played were doubtless far too courtly to carry victory unpleasantly far.

—GEORGE WALKER, *Chess and Chessplayers*

Surely chess is a sad waste of brains.

—SIR WALTER SCOTT

What chess has in common with science and fine art is its utter uselessness.

—ERNST CASSIRER

Once upon a time, during one of the Hungarian championships, Balla was playing Breyer. Both players were hunched over the board. Suddenly Balla looked up excitedly: "Mate in two!" he crowed. The spectators all stared at Breyer. He looked rather bored, but otherwise showed no reaction. Astonished, Balla stared at the position again, and to his horror, he found that the mate in two didn't exist.

However, after further study, he found the solution. "Mate in three!" he shouted, more excited than ever. But Breyer still looked bored. Crestfallen, Balla turned back to the position, grew pale . . . there was no mate in three either!! What to do? He studied and studied and studied. Suddenly he came to a conclusion . . . the spectators hung on his words. . . . "I resign," he whispered.

Rubber checkmate!

—I. A. HOROWITZ, *Chess Review*, 1946

I have known a person consume an hour in looking over a game at Chess, without understanding the Moves.

—*The Looker-on*, 1792

Memory, rather than intelligence, is the most important factor in chess playing.

—C. A. CLAREMONT, *The Chemistry of Thought*, 1935

When Labourdonnais [about 1835] was requested by a French publisher to prepare an elementary work on chess, the author wrote with a shovel instead of a pen; that is, he carted into his book large extracts from Philidor and George Walker. Indeed, the book fell still-born from the press. I cannot imagine Labourdonnais as a teacher.

He was too fiery and impatient. His place was at the chessboard, playing games at various odds by the score, and marking the number by pegging the holes which he had ordered to be made in the frame of the board. After playing a match game from which McDonnell would retire exhausted, the more vigorous antagonist would sit up for hours, accomplishing the above feat, and drinking *bière à la portère*.

— CHARLES TOMLINSON, *British Chess Magazine*, 1891

I got in a position where only a desperate maneuver could save me. Tarrasch had outplayed me in the opening, but he lacked the passion that whips the blood when great stakes can be gained by resolute and self-confident daring.

— EMANUEL LASKER, *American Chess Bulletin*, 1908

Colonel Stewart used frequently to play at Chess with Lord Stair (whose A.D.C. he was), who was very fond of the game; but an unexpected checkmate used to put his Lordship into such a passion that he was ready to throw a candlestick, or anything else that was near him, at his adversary; for which reason the Colonel always took care to be on his feet, to fly to the furthest corner of the room, when he said, "Checkmate, my Lord."

— RICHARD TWISS, *Chess*, 1787

It will be cheering to know that many people are skillful chess players, though in many instances their brains, in a general way, compare unfavorably with the cogitative faculties of a rabbit.

— JAMES MORTIMER

Chess is a form of intellectual productiveness; therein lies its peculiar charm. Intellectual productiveness is one of the greatest joys—if not the greatest one—of human existence. It is not everyone who can write a play, or build a bridge, or even make a good joke. But in chess everyone can, everyone must, be intellectually productive, and so can share in this select delight. I have always a slight feeling of pity for the man who has no knowledge of chess, just as I would pity the man who has remained ignorant of love. Chess, like love, like music, has the power to make men happy.

— SIEGBERT TARRASCH